The 39 Steps
Play Guide

for AQA GCSE Drama

Annie Fox

Published in 2019 by Illuminate Publishing Ltd, P.O. Box 1160, Cheltenham, Gloucestershire GL50 9RW

Orders: Please visit www.illuminatepublishing.com or email sales@illuminatepublishing.com

British Library Cataloguing in Publication Data

A catalogue record for this book is available from the British Library.

ISBN 978 1 911208 72 3

Printed in the UK by Cambrian Printers, Aberystwyth

03.19

The publisher's policy is to use papers that are natural, renewable and recyclable products made from wood grown in sustainable forests. The logging and manufacturing processes are expected to conform to the environmental regulations of the country of origin.

Every effort has been made to contact copyright holders of material reproduced in this book. Great care has been taken by the author and publishers to ensure that either formal permission has been granted for the use of copyright material reproduced, or that copyright material has been used under fair-dealing guidelines in the UK – specifically that it has been used sparingly, for the purpose of criticism and review, and has been properly acknowledged. If notified, the publishers will be pleased to rectify any errors or omissions at the earliest opportunity.

Editor: Roanne Charles, abc Editorial
Design and layout: Neil Sutton, Cambridge Design Consultants
Cover design: Neil Sutton, Cambridge Design Consultants. Cover photograph: WENN Ltd / Alamy Stock Photo

Text acknowledgements

Extracts in this book are taken from *The 39 Steps* Acting Edition by John Buchan adapted by Patrick Barlow, published by Samuel French.

Page 86 extract from 'Summer and Smoke, Almeida Theatre, London, review' by Holly Williams © *Independent*, 8 March 2018; extract from 'Review: Summer and Smoke' by Daisy Bowie-Sell reproduced with the kind permission of WhatsOnStage.com.

Picture acknowledgements

pp4 bottom and 104 Broadway.com; pp6–8, 13 left, 14 right, 15 top, 16 top, 17 top, 18 top, 20, 21, 28, 32 top, 41, 46 top, 66, 80 top, 81–82, 84, 94, 98, 100, 110, 124 top, 129, 144 and 146 emc design; pp11, 37, 68–69 and 139 Neil Sutton; pp12 **1** and **2**, 92, 93 left, 107, 108 top and bottom, 115, 116, 120 and 124 bottom © Paul Fox; p12 **3** Joan Marcus; p13 right Tony Bartholemew; pp14 left and 19 Granger Historical Picture Archive / Alamy Stock Photo; p15 bottom Sheffield Theatres; p16 bottom King's Cross Theatre; p17 bottom Richard Lakos; p18 bottom Robin Roemer; p22 Criterion Theatre; pp30 top, 31, 46 top and bottom and 56 Everett Collection Inc / Alamy Stock Photo, p26 Harlequin Productions; p30 bottom Glasshouse Images / Alamy Stock Photo; p32 bottom ClassicStock / Alamy Stock Photo; p33 Chronicle / Alamy Stock Photo; p34 INTERFOTO / Alamy Stock Photo; pp35 left and 38 Pictorial Press / Alamy Stock Photo; p35 centre Blanche Rothschild, right digitalheritage.org; p36 left G.W. French, right D and S Photography Archives / Alamy Stock Photo, bottom Jan Fehribach; p39 left wales_heritage_photos / Alamy Stock Photo, right Ian Dagnell / Alamy Stock Photo; p40 right tripadvisor; p42 Londonstills.com / Alamy Stock Photo; pp43 and 60 left Alistair Muir / Peter McKintosh; p46 centre Moviestore collection Ltd / Alamy Stock Photo; p48 ITV Studios; pp52 and 60 top Dan Tsantilis; p53 Tracy Martin; p57 MGM; p58 William Marsh; pp59 and 62 Sam Taylor; p60 bottom Mark Kitaoka; p67 Stan Barouh; p73 Matthew Gilmore; p80 bottom Burt Vanderveen; pp90 and 136 Alastair Muir; pp93 right and 95 Marc Brenner; p93 bottom Helen Murray; p96 Geraint Lewis / Alamy Stock Photo; p99 Sueddeutsche Zeitung Photo / Alamy Stock Photo; p102 Manuel Harlan; p108 right © Steve Tanner / Kneehigh; p117 Johan Persson; p125 Bettina Strenske / Alamy Stock Photo.

All other images **Shutterstock**:
p4 top Iakov Filimonov; p39 top Hugh McKean; p40 left Electric Egg / Shutterstock.com; p83 vichie81; p105 top left Pavel L Photo and Video / Shutterstock.com, top right criben/Shutterstock.com, bottom left evgenii mitroshin, bottom right Oleinik Iuliia / Shutterstock.com; p119 Tito Wong; p122 Bata Zivanovic; p123 Feng Yu; pp126–127 agusyonok; p132 Monkey Business Images; p140 Nukul Chanada.

CONTENTS

INTRODUCTION

This Play Guide is designed to help you to succeed in all aspects of Component 1 of AQA GCSE Drama, focusing on *The 39 Steps* by John Buchan and Patrick Barlow as your set text for Section B. You might use the book alongside the work you are doing in your lessons at school or to help you with your independent revision. Throughout this book, there are creative tasks, sample exam questions and suggested answers, as well as helpful opportunities to check and stretch your learning.

What is Component 1?

Component 1 of GCSE Drama is 'Understanding drama'. The exam is a written one that consists of three sections, with a total of 80 marks:

▸ Section A: Theatre roles and terminology (4 marks)
▸ Section B: Study of a set text (44 marks)
▸ Section C: Live theatre production (32 marks).

It accounts for 40 per cent of the GCSE Drama assessment. (The remainder being the practical components 'Devising drama' and 'Texts in practice'.)

How are you assessed?

The exam assesses your:
▸ Knowledge and understanding of drama and theatre
▸ Study of one set play (from a choice of six)
▸ Analysis and evaluation of the work of live theatre makers.

Section A: Theatre roles and terminology

This part of the exam consists of multiple-choice questions on topics such as the:
▸ Roles and responsibilities of theatre makers
▸ Features of different staging configurations
▸ Correct terms for different positions on stage.

Section B: Study of a set text

This section contains questions about the particular set text you have studied. You will be presented with an extract from the set play. The first three questions are compulsory for all students, then you will need to choose to answer either the fourth or fifth question. Topics covered typically include:
▸ Using design to convey the context of the play
▸ Vocal and physical performance skills
▸ Use of stage space and interaction between characters
▸ One question with a choice of performance or design specialism.

You will need to write paragraphs in response to these questions, although you might also, if you choose, include sketches to support your design ideas. You should aim for well-organised responses that use specialist vocabulary appropriately.

Section C: Live theatre production

Section C consists of three questions. You will choose one to answer in reference to a live drama production. The questions will ask you to describe, analyse and evaluate either a performance aspect or design aspect of the production you have seen.

How to use this book

This book is designed to cover all aspects of Component 1 for those studying *The 39 Steps* as their set text. There are chapters devoted to each section of the written exam, as well as a chapter on improving your writing and exam skills. There is also a glossary that provides a useful reference and will help you to improve your use of technical terms. There are many examples of exam-style questions for you to practise essay writing and other responses within time limits.

You may choose to work through the book in any order that you like, but, to make full use of the guidance and ideas offered for the whole exam, make sure you cover all sections. There is a crossover in the different skills developed in the various sections, so that you might find, for example, the technical vocabulary explained in Section C helpful to your writing in Section B. Understanding the different staging configurations and positions explained in Section A might also be helpful when writing about design or performances in Sections B and C.

Some special features to help you get the most from the book include:

 Tips: Guidance for the exam and how to avoid common errors.

Tasks: Practical activities to improve your learning. These include, for example, experimenting with acting skills on particular extracts, sketching costume and set designs or evaluating sample answers.

Key terms: Definitions of drama vocabulary to help you understand how drama works and to express your ideas fluently and appropriately. These are also gathered in a glossary at the back of the book as a reference resource.

 Test yourself: A set of quick questions that revise key ideas and terms covered in the preceding guidance pages.

Learning checklist: A review at the end of a topic in which you can assess your learning and decide which areas require more revision.

What the specification says: Notes on the assessment objectives and the demands of the specification.

Practice questions: A range of exam-style questions for you to attempt, ideally under exam-type conditions.

Sample answers: Candidate-style responses to exam-type questions, annotated to show where marks might be gained or lost.

 Look here: Suggestions on where you can find more information about a given topic elsewhere in this book.

 Check it out: References to the *AQA GCSE Drama* coursebook, for additional information and details.

 Pages that are available to download and print as worksheets from www.illuminatepublishing.com/drama.

 TIP

Be aware of how many marks different questions are worth and organise your revision appropriately. A good approach is to spend the most time preparing for the questions worth the most marks.

 TIP

If you need more assistance with the course, including Components 2 and 3, try the accompanying *AQA GCSE Drama* book, which covers all the set texts and all the components of the AQA GCSE Drama course.

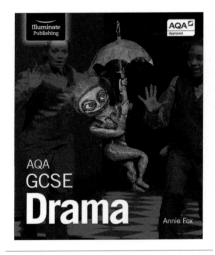

 **TEST YOURSELF 1**

1 In which section of the exam will you write about a live theatre production you have seen?

2 How many questions in total are you required to answer in Section B?

3 Which section of the exam (A, B or C) is worth the most marks?

4 The written exam is worth what percentage of your Drama GCSE?

5 Which section of the exam consists of multiple-choice questions?

6 Besides the 'key terms' notes, where in this book will you find definitions of drama vocabulary?

THEATRE ROLES AND TERMINOLOGY

Assessment focus:

AO3: Demonstrate knowledge and understanding of how drama and theatre are developed and performed.

What the specification says...

The specification requires you to have knowledge of how theatre works in a practical way. In order to express yourself accurately when writing about drama, you need to understand:

▶ the different ways plays could be staged

▶ what the advantages and challenges of different theatre configurations are

▶ who is responsible for different elements of a production.

Students must develop knowledge and understanding of:

▶ Drama and theatre terminology and how to use it appropriately:

— stage positioning

— staging configurations.

Students should have a general understanding of the implications of the above stage configurations on the use of the performance space.

▶ The roles and responsibilities of theatre makers in contemporary professional practice. Knowledge and understanding should cover:

— the activities each might undertake on a day-to-day basis

— the aspects of the rehearsal/performance process each is accountable for (their contribution to the whole production being a success).

You will be assessed by:

▶ multiple-choice questions.

The names and roles of theatre makers

Many different people are involved with creating a successful production of a theatrical performance. Key people whose roles you should understand include:

PLAYWRIGHT

Writes the script of the play, including dialogue and stage directions.

PERFORMER

Appears in a production, for example, acting, dancing or singing.

Creates a performance or assumes a role on stage in front of an audience.

DIRECTOR

Oversees and manages the creative aspects of the production.

Develops a 'concept' or central unifying idea for the production.

Liaises with designers, rehearses the performers and ensures that all elements of the production are ready.

Blocks the movements of the actors and gives 'notes' to improve performances.

THEATRE MANAGER

In charge of the theatre building, including overseeing the front of house and box office staff who sell tickets and liaise with the public.

UNDERSTUDY

Learns a part, including lines and movements, so they are able to take over a role for someone, if needed, when there is a planned or unexpected absence.

STAGE MANAGER

Runs the backstage elements of the play, and supervises the backstage crew.

Organises the rehearsal schedule and keeps lists of props and other technical needs.

Creates a prompt book and calls the cues for the performance.

TECHNICIAN

Operates the technical equipment, such as lighting and sound boards, during the performance.

SOUND DESIGNER

Designs the sound required for the performance, which might include music and sound effects.

Creates a sound plot.

Takes appropriate action if amplification, such as the use of microphones, is needed.

LIGHTING DESIGNER

Designs the lighting states and effects that will be used in a performance.

Understands the technical capabilities of the theatre and creates a lighting plot accordingly.

COSTUME DESIGNER

Designs what the actors wear on stage.

Provides sketches and other design materials.

Ensures that costumes are appropriate for the play and fit the performers.

SET DESIGNER

Designs the set and, if needed, the set dressings (objects placed on the stage).

Provides sketches and other design materials, before overseeing the creation of the set.

PUPPET DESIGNER

Designs the puppets for a production, as needed, taking into account the style of the puppets and how they will be operated.

KEY TERMS

Block: Set the movements made by the actors.

Front of house: Ushers and other members of theatre staff who deal with the audience, as opposed to those who work backstage.

Props: Small items that actors can carry, such as books, a pistol or a bottle.

Prompt book: A copy of the production script of the play, which includes detailed information about the play's blocking, props and other technical elements.

Call the cues: Announce instructions, for example telling technicians when lighting or sound changes should occur.

Sound plot: A list of the sound effects or music needed and sound equipment that will be used. This is usually organised scene-by-scene and contains information such as cues and volume.

Amplification: How sounds are made louder, usually through the use of microphones or other sound-boosting equipment.

Lighting states: The settings and positions of lighting to create certain lighting conditions, such as a bright afternoon or a moonlit scene.

Lighting plot: A guide to the lighting of a production, including the locations and types of various lighting instruments and a scene-by-scene list of lighting requirements.

Who is responsible for what and when in theatre making?

- ▸ Stage manager and technicians are hired.

- ▸ Once cast, performers begin to prepare their roles.

- ▸ The director decides on the **concept** of the production and casts the performers.

- ▸ The playwright produces a script.

- ▸ Designers produce initial designs — for sets, costumes and lighting, for example — and begin any pre-production work.

- ▸ The theatre manager agrees the use of theatre and prepares it for the production.

BEFORE REHEARSALS

- ▸ The theatre manager ensures the theatre will be ready and relevant staff are hired.

- ▸ Designers realise their designs, including costume fittings, set construction and lighting plots.

- ▸ Understudies learn the role or roles they are **covering**.

- ▸ Performers rehearse their roles, learn lines and blocking.

- ▸ The stage manager notes the blocking, creates rehearsal lists and prepares the prompt book.

DURING REHEARSALS

- ▸ The director leads rehearsals with performers.

DURING PERFORMANCES

- ▸ The theatre manager ensures front of house is run smoothly.

- ▸ The stage manager runs the show, using the prompt book, and calls the cues.

- ▸ Understudies are prepared to go on stage if a performer is unable to.

- ▸ Technicians operate technical equipment, such as sound and lighting boards.

- ▸ Performers present their roles before an audience.

TIP

Some productions will vary from the typical roles and responsibilities listed on these two pages. For example, some shows don't start with a script, but are devised as they go along. In some productions, members of the cast also take on backstage roles or the direction of the play. The exam, however, will be based on the typical division of responsibilities as explained here.

KEY TERMS

Concept: A unifying idea about the production, such as how it will be interpreted and performed.

Covering (a role): Learning the lines and movements for a part that you do not usually perform.

CHECK IT OUT

See page 18 of *AQA GCSE Drama* for three short interviews in which theatre makers discuss their roles.

TEST YOURSELF A1

Look at the descriptions below of various theatre makers describing their roles and responsibilities. Match each description with the correct theatre maker.

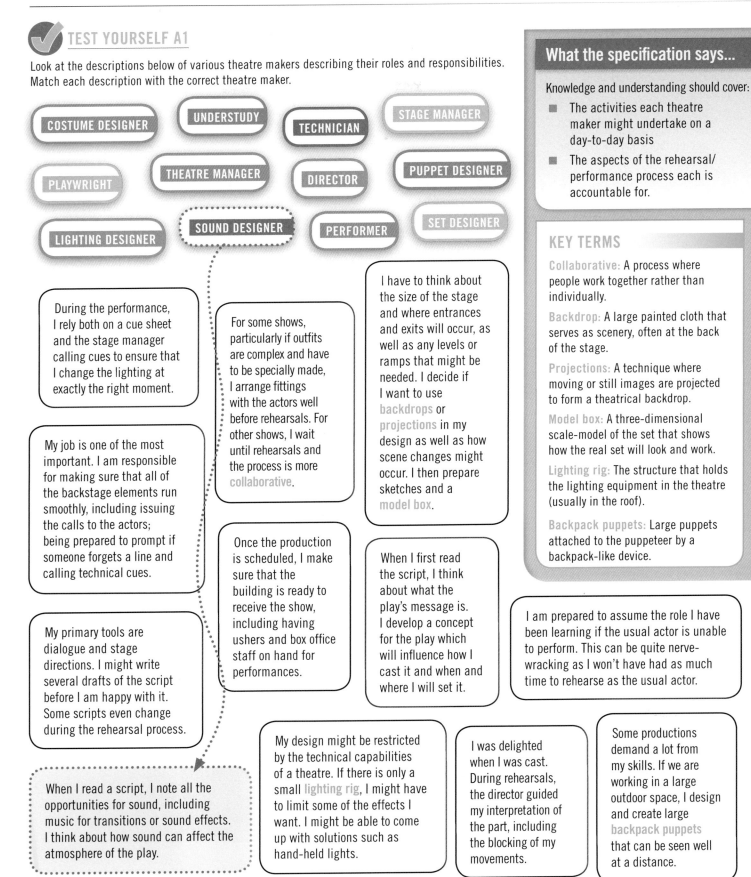

COSTUME DESIGNER

UNDERSTUDY

TECHNICIAN

STAGE MANAGER

PLAYWRIGHT

THEATRE MANAGER

DIRECTOR

PUPPET DESIGNER

LIGHTING DESIGNER

SOUND DESIGNER

PERFORMER

SET DESIGNER

During the performance, I rely both on a cue sheet and the stage manager calling cues to ensure that I change the lighting at exactly the right moment.

My job is one of the most important. I am responsible for making sure that all of the backstage elements run smoothly, including issuing the calls to the actors; being prepared to prompt if someone forgets a line and calling technical cues.

My primary tools are dialogue and stage directions. I might write several drafts of the script before I am happy with it. Some scripts even change during the rehearsal process.

When I read a script, I note all the opportunities for sound, including music for transitions or sound effects. I think about how sound can affect the atmosphere of the play.

For some shows, particularly if outfits are complex and have to be specially made, I arrange fittings with the actors well before rehearsals. For other shows, I wait until rehearsals and the process is more collaborative.

Once the production is scheduled, I make sure that the building is ready to receive the show, including having ushers and box office staff on hand for performances.

My design might be restricted by the technical capabilities of a theatre. If there is only a small lighting rig, I might have to limit some of the effects I want. I might be able to come up with solutions such as hand-held lights.

I have to think about the size of the stage and where entrances and exits will occur, as well as any levels or ramps that might be needed. I decide if I want to use backdrops or projections in my design as well as how scene changes might occur. I then prepare sketches and a model box.

When I first read the script, I think about what the play's message is. I develop a concept for the play which will influence how I cast it and when and where I will set it.

I was delighted when I was cast. During rehearsals, the director guided my interpretation of the part, including the blocking of my movements.

I am prepared to assume the role I have been learning if the usual actor is unable to perform. This can be quite nerve-wracking as I won't have had as much time to rehearse as the usual actor.

Some productions demand a lot from my skills. If we are working in a large outdoor space, I design and create large backpack puppets that can be seen well at a distance.

What the specification says...

Knowledge and understanding should cover:

- The activities each theatre maker might undertake on a day-to-day basis
- The aspects of the rehearsal/performance process each is accountable for.

KEY TERMS

Collaborative: A process where people work together rather than individually.

Backdrop: A large painted cloth that serves as scenery, often at the back of the stage.

Projections: A technique where moving or still images are projected to form a theatrical backdrop.

Model box: A three-dimensional scale-model of the set that shows how the real set will look and work.

Lighting rig: The structure that holds the lighting equipment in the theatre (usually in the roof).

Backpack puppets: Large puppets attached to the puppeteer by a backpack-like device.

Stage positioning

In order to note movements in a script or to express locations quickly, theatre makers use subject-specific terminology to describe places on the stage.

The diagram below shows the stage positions of a typical rectangular **end on staging configuration**.

 TIP

To understand if you need to refer to 'right' or 'left,' imagine you are an actor standing on the centre of the stage, facing the audience. Stage right is to your right and stage left is to your left. The left and right refer to the actor's left and right, not the audience's.

KEY TERMS

End on: A staging configuration in which the audience sits along one end of the stage (the front), directly facing it.

Staging configuration: The type of stage and audience arrangement.

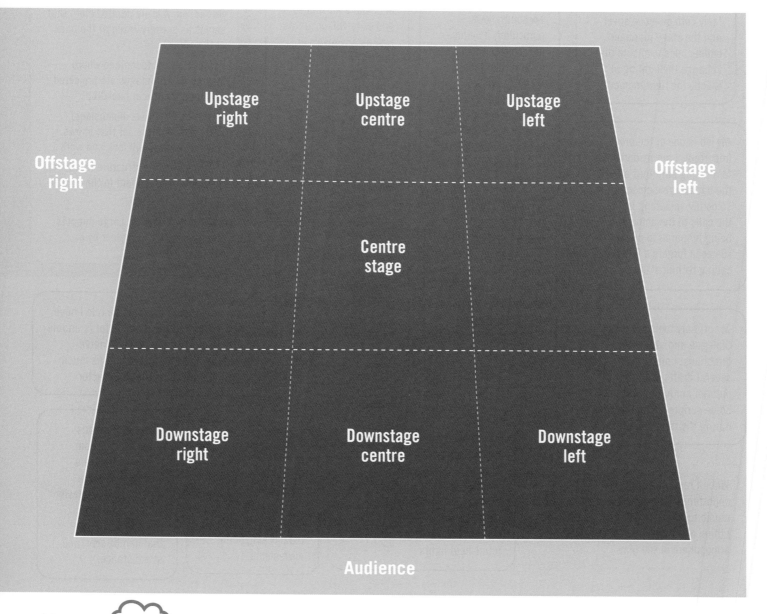

TASK A1

1 Imagine you are a set designer and the director has asked you to put the following items on stage:

    A A wide doorway, upstage centre

    B A pair of chairs and a table, centre stage

    C A small rug, downstage right

    D A window, upstage left

    E A kitchen sink, stage right.

Use the diagram on the previous page to note where you would put them.

TIP

When describing where characters are in relation to each other, you can use the same stage-positioning terminology. For example, if you have one character standing behind another and they are both facing downstage, you could say that the character behind is standing *upstage* of the other one. If you want a character to move from upstage right to downstage left, you could write that they *cross downstage left*.

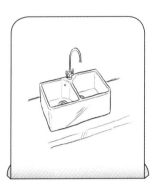

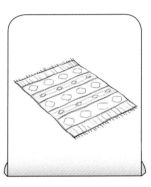

2 Now imagine you are an actor and you have been asked to do the following blocking. Note where on the stage you will be each time.

    A Enter through the wide doorway.

    B Make yourself a cup of tea.

    C Sit down on a chair.

    D Look dreamily out of the window.

    E Stand as close and centrally to the audience as you can.

    F Move as far away from the small rug as you can.

3 Copy a new version of the stage space and decide where you would position the characters at the beginning of Scene 13 in the Crofter's Cottage, when Margaret is showing Hannay the room. After you have marked where the characters and furniture are positioned, annotate the diagram by describing their stage positions. For example, if you have put Hannay downstage, you might write: *Hannay: downstage left* (or DSL).

Staging configuration

When deciding which staging configuration is best suited to a particular production, some considerations might be:

▶ Whether there is space to store large pieces of scenery to the side of the stage (wings) or above the stage
▶ How scene/set changes will be accomplished
▶ Whether you need curtains to hide scene changes or to create particular effects
▶ How close you want the audience to be to the action
▶ How formal a setting you want
▶ Where entrances and exits will take place
▶ Whether there is any audience interaction
▶ The style and size of your set and its desired effect
▶ Whether it matters if the audience can see one another
▶ Whether you want the audience to move with the action
▶ How important it is for all audience members to see the play from the same perspective
▶ The types of performance the actors will be giving.

 TEST YOURSELF A2

Before you read on for details about staging, try to identify the type of stage configuration in each image below. How can you tell?

1

2

TIP

As you learn about the various staging configurations, think about the advantages and disadvantages of each, as well as the different types of performance that they might suit.

3

Theatre in the round

Theatre in the round is a staging configuration where the audience is seated around all sides of the centrally placed stage.

Theatre in the round ▼

Task A2

The Stephen Joseph Theatre in Scarborough is a well-known example of a theatre in the round. Look at this photograph from its production of *Confusions* by Alan Ayckbourn. What are the challenges for the set designer and actors of using this configuration?

Stephen Joseph Theatre, Scarborough ▼

Advantages:

▸ It often suits productions where the audience should be close to the action.

▸ It can encourage **audience interaction** and/or a sense of intimacy.

▸ Entrances and exits are usually made through the audience, which can be exciting.

▸ The audience might feel more involved with the action as there is no obvious '**fourth wall**'.

Challenges:

▸ Blocking must be done carefully, so that certain sections of the audience don't miss key moments of action or dialogue, or facial expressions.

▸ Tall **flats**, backdrops or stage furniture cannot be used, as they will restrict **sightlines**.

▸ The audience can see each other, which can be distracting.

▸ It can be difficult to create a single '**stage picture**' which is sufficiently effective for the whole audience.

▸ It is difficult to put a curtain around the stage, so scene changes might have to occur within the view of the audience.

KEY TERMS

Audience interaction: Directly involving members of the audience in the play, for example by bringing them onstage, going into the audience to speak with them, asking for a response from onstage, or passing them props to hold.

Fourth wall: An imaginary wall that separates the actors from the audience, giving the impression that the world of the actors is entirely distinct from that of the audience.

Flats: Pieces of scenery mounted on frames, for example representing walls.

Sightlines: The view the audience has of the stage and/or dramatic action. If a sightline is blocked or restricted, for example by a poorly placed piece of furniture, it means that some audience members cannot see part of the stage.

Stage picture: A well-arranged visual stage image that conveys a certain impression to the audience; also called a 'tableau'.

Task A3

A famous example of a proscenium arch is in the Royal Opera House in London. Imagine you have been asked to stage Scene 2 (Cockney Musical Hall) of *The 39 Steps* in this configuration. Write a paragraph describing how you would use this staging. Include use of:

- Wings/fly space
- Curtains
- Apron space
- Entrances and exits.

The proscenium arch of the Royal Opera House, Covent Garden ▾

KEY TERMS

Apron: The front area of the stage, nearest the audience, which projects in front of the curtain.

Fly space: The area above the stage where scenery might be stored and lowered to the stage.

Wing space: An area to the side of the stage. This is the space where actors, unseen by the audience, wait to enter and where props and set pieces can be stored.

Proscenium arch stage

A proscenium arch theatre is one of the most common forms of theatre, especially for larger, more formal theatres and opera houses. The proscenium refers to the frame around the stage, which emphasises that the whole audience is seeing the same stage picture. The area in front of the arch is called an **apron**. This is the stage area nearest the audience in front of the curtain.

A proscenium arch stage ▴

Advantages:

- ▸ The proscenium frame emphasises the stage pictures.
- ▸ Backdrops and large scenery can be used without interfering with sightlines.
- ▸ There might be **fly space** and **wing spaces** for storing scenery.
- ▸ The frame around the stage adds to the effect of the fourth wall, giving the impression of a self-contained world.
- ▸ When the curtains are down, for example for set changes, scenes might be played in front of the curtain on the stage's apron.

Challenges:

- ▸ Some audience members might feel distant from the stage.
- ▸ The auditorium might feel very formal and rigid.
- ▸ The proscenium frame might seem too old-fashioned to some.
- ▸ Audience interaction might be more difficult.

Thrust stage

A thrust stage juts into the auditorium, with the audience arranged on three sides. This is one of the oldest types of theatre stage. Ancient Greek amphitheatres (where the audience was seated in a semicircle around almost half the curved stage) and the theatres in Shakespeare's day (where the audience in the pit stood around three sides of the stage) are both types of thrust stages. In the mid-20th century, they became an increasingly popular staging configuration again, and are used in theatres such as the Crucible Theatre in Sheffield, built in 1971.

A thrust stage ▲

Task A4

Imagine you have been asked to stage Scene 27 (Hotel Bedroom) from *The 39 Steps* (pages 66–67) on a thrust stage. Draw an outline of a thrust staging configuration and mark on it of where you would place the scenery and actors. Remember to consider audience sightlines and the effects you wish to create.

Advantages:

▸ It combines some of the benefits of both proscenium and theatre-in-the-round stages.

▸ As there is no audience on the upstage side of the stage, backdrops, flats, projections and large scenery can be used.

▸ Many members of the audience might feel closer to the performance as there are three first rows – one on each of the stage's three sides – and they are often close to the edge of the stage.

▸ This is often perceived as an exciting performance space that encourages a connection between the performers and the audience.

Challenges:

▸ Sightlines for those on the extreme sides might be restricted or obstructed.

▸ The audience on the right and left sides of the auditorium have each other in their view.

▸ Box sets – where three sides of a room are constructed – cannot be used as they would restrict views for much of the audience.

▸ Not all of the audience members see the stage from the same angle, so stage pictures might be more difficult to create.

The Crucible Theatre, Sheffield ▼

KEY TERM

Box set: A set with three complete walls, often used in naturalistic set designs, for example to create a believable room.

Traverse stage

A traverse stage has a long central acting area. The audience is seated on either side of this playing area, facing each other. Although it is relatively rare for a traverse stage to be the permanent staging configuration for a theatre, some flexible theatres rearrange their auditoriums to create this configuration.

> ### Task A5
>
> Make a list of locations which you believe would particularly suit a traverse staging configuration.

A traverse stage ▲

Advantages:

- Many audience members will feel very close to the action, as there are two long front rows.
- The audience can see the reactions of the other people facing them. This might increase a feeling of involvement and interaction.
- It can be used to recreate certain settings with great effect, such as a catwalk, a pavement, a conveyor belt or a railway platform.
- The extreme ends of the stage can be used to create additional acting areas.

Challenges:

- Large pieces of scenery, stage furniture or backdrops can block sightlines.
- The long, thin nature of the acting area can make some blocking tricky.
- Actors must be aware of making themselves visible and audible to both sides of the audience.
- Lighting needs to be arranged carefully to avoid lights shining into the audience's eyes or spilling onto them.
- Some audience members might find being able to see each other distracting and unsettling.

The Railway Children *at King's Cross Theatre* ▼

End on staging

With end on staging, the audience is seated along one end of the stage, directly facing it. This is similar to a proscenium arch stage, but without the large proscenium frame.

End on staging ▲

Four Play at Theatre 503 ▼

Advantages:

▶ The audience members all have a similar view.

▶ Stage pictures are easy to create.

▶ Large backdrops, projections and box sets can be used.

Challenges:

▶ Audience members at the back might feel distant from the action.

▶ It doesn't have the decorative frame of a proscenium arch theatre and possibly will not have the curtains, which give flexibility in some productions.

▶ The stage might not have the wing and fly spaces associated with large proscenium arch theatres.

Promenade theatre in a town square ▲

KEY TERM

Immersive: A type of theatre where the audience are in the middle of the action, without the sense of separation usually associated with going to the theatre. They might be required to wear masks, costumes or to follow certain characters.

Promenade

Promenade theatre is a performance setting where there is no formal, separate stage. Instead, the audience members stand or follow the actors through the performance. This might occur in a conventional theatre space, but often promenade productions take place in larger, unconventional spaces such as parks, warehouses or office spaces. Theatre companies such as Punchdrunk and dreamthinkspeak are famous for their innovative and **immersive** promenade productions.

Punchdrunk's Sleep No More, *New York – the audience members are wearing masks.* ▼

Advantages:

▶ There can be exciting design opportunities in converting an unusual space into a performance area.

▶ This is an interactive and exciting type of theatre, where the audience can feel very involved.

▶ This type of staging is likely to enable experimental and new types of theatre.

Challenges:

▶ The audience might find moving around the space difficult or get tired of standing.

▶ Actors or stage crew need to be skilled at moving the audience around and controlling their focus.

▶ There can be technical challenges in ensuring that all audience members can see and hear the action.

▶ There can be health and safety risks.

✓ TEST YOURSELF A3

Read the descriptions of different staging configurations below and decide which is being described:

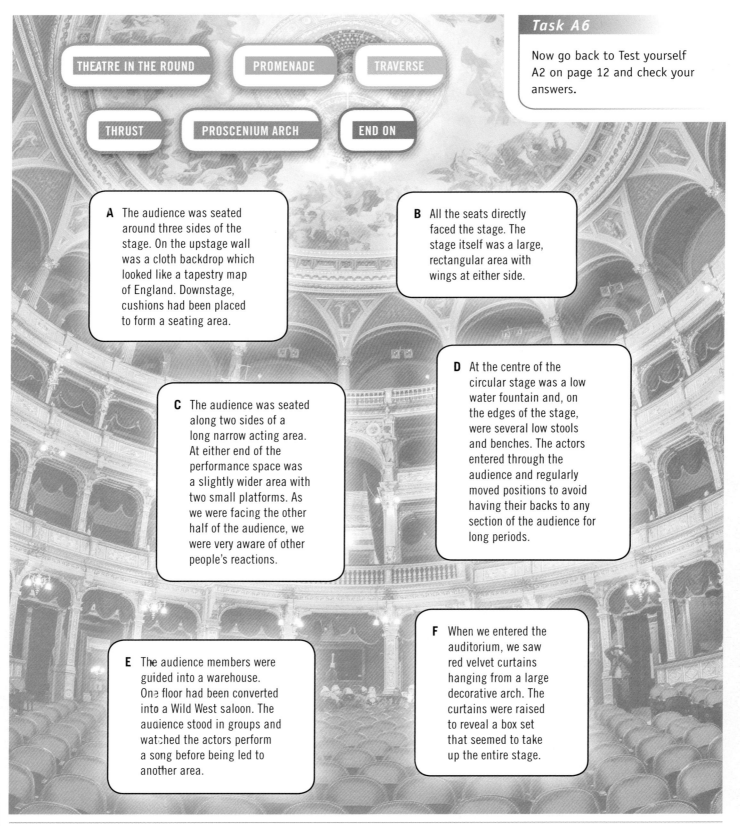

THEATRE IN THE ROUND   PROMENADE   TRAVERSE

THRUST   PROSCENIUM ARCH   END ON

Task A6

Now go back to Test yourself A2 on page 12 and check your answers.

A The audience was seated around three sides of the stage. On the upstage wall was a cloth backdrop which looked like a tapestry map of England. Downstage, cushions had been placed to form a seating area.

B All the seats directly faced the stage. The stage itself was a large, rectangular area with wings at either side.

C The audience was seated along two sides of a long narrow acting area. At either end of the performance space was a slightly wider area with two small platforms. As we were facing the other half of the audience, we were very aware of other people's reactions.

D At the centre of the circular stage was a low water fountain and, on the edges of the stage, were several low stools and benches. The actors entered through the audience and regularly moved positions to avoid having their backs to any section of the audience for long periods.

E The audience members were guided into a warehouse. One floor had been converted into a Wild West saloon. The audience stood in groups and watched the actors perform a song before being led to another area.

F When we entered the auditorium, we saw red velvet curtains hanging from a large decorative arch. The curtains were raised to reveal a box set that seemed to take up the entire stage.

Practice questions for Section A

You will answer a number of multiple-choice questions in your exam.

Part 1

1 In professional theatre, who is responsible for calling the cues during a show?

    A The theatre manager.

    B The stage manager.

    C The director.

2 When performing in a theatre in the round, which of the following is true?

    A The audience is encouraged to stand and walk around.

    B The audience is arranged on all sides of the playing space.

    C It is easy to use large pieces of scenery or backdrops.

3 What type of stage is shown in this diagram?

    A A thrust stage.

    B A traverse stage.

    C A proscenium arch.

4 With reference to the stage in Question 3, in what position is the table?

    A Downstage left.

    B Downstage right.

    C Upstage left.

Part 2

1 In professional theatre, who is responsible for running the theatre building, including making sure it is safe for audience and performers, and ready for the production?

    A The technician.

    B The stage manager.

    C The theatre manager.

2 Which of the following configurations is best suited for a play where you want the actors to enter and exit through the audience and for the audience to be sitting all around the stage space?

    A Theatre in the round.

    B Proscenium arch.

    C End on.

3 What type of stage is shown here?

    A Promenade theatre.

    B Thrust theatre.

    C Proscenium arch theatre.

4 With reference to the stage in Question 3, what stage position is the microphone in?

    A Downstage left.

    B Centre stage.

    C Upstage centre.

LEARNING CHECKLIST: SECTION A

Tick each aspect of theatre roles and terminology if you are confident of your knowledge.

If you are unsure of anything, go back and revise.

Do you know...?

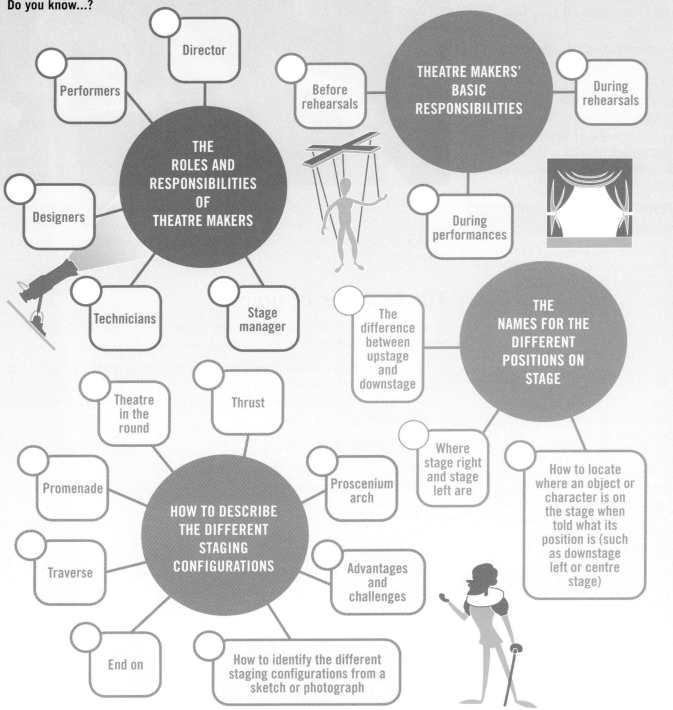

- Director
- Performers
- Before rehearsals
- THEATRE MAKERS' BASIC RESPONSIBILITIES
- During rehearsals
- THE ROLES AND RESPONSIBILITIES OF THEATRE MAKERS
- Designers
- During performances
- Technicians
- Stage manager
- The difference between upstage and downstage
- THE NAMES FOR THE DIFFERENT POSITIONS ON STAGE
- Theatre in the round
- Thrust
- Where stage right and stage left are
- Promenade
- Proscenium arch
- How to locate where an object or character is on the stage when told what its position is (such as downstage left or centre stage)
- HOW TO DESCRIBE THE DIFFERENT STAGING CONFIGURATIONS
- Traverse
- Advantages and challenges
- End on
- How to identify the different staging configurations from a sketch or photograph

STUDY OF A SET PLAY: THE 39 STEPS

Ben Righton and Ellie Beaven star in the Criterion Theatre production

What the specification says...

Students are expected to know and understand:

▶ the characteristics and context of the whole play they have studied.

One extract from each set play is printed in the question paper.

Students answer questions relating to that extract, referring to the whole play as appropriate to the demands of the question.

Assessment focus:

AO3: Demonstrate knowledge and understanding of how drama and theatre are developed and performed.

For Component 1, Section B, you will study one of six set plays. One of these set plays is *The 39 Steps*, adapted by Patrick Barlow, which is covered in detail in this chapter. All page numbers given refer to the Samuel French edition of the play (ISBN 978-0-573-11440-3).

The features of drama

In Section B, you will have the opportunity to share your understanding of *The 39 Steps* and your ideas about how it could be performed and designed.

Writing about drama is different from writing an English Literature essay. In Drama, you are expected to demonstrate a **practical** understanding of how acting and design choices can create a particular **interpretation** of a text and how those choices will have an impact on the audience.

Characteristics of a play

▶ Genre   ▶ Style
▶ Plot   ▶ Characters.

Context

▶ The time period in which the play is set.
▶ The location of the play.
▶ The political or social concerns expressed in the play.
▶ The clothing and furnishing fashions of the time.
▶ The educational, artistic and other cultural factors of the time.
▶ The backgrounds of the characters.

Examples of practical understanding

▶ How a play could be acted, including physical and vocal skills.
▶ How it could be staged, including staging configuration and placement of characters on stage.
▶ How it could be designed, including costumes, set, props, lighting and sound.

KEY TERMS

Practical: Something that can actually be physically done, rather than simply an idea.

Interpretation: Bringing out a particular meaning by making specific choices. In this case, how a play could be performed or designed in order to get across a particular meaning. There might be many possible interpretations.

Genre: A category or type of music, art or literature, usually with its own typical conventions.

Plot: The sequence of main events of a play, film or novel.

Style: The way in which something is created or performed.

Characters: The people involved in the action of a play, film or novel.

TEST YOURSELF B1

Match the theatrical term with its correct application to *The 39 Steps*.

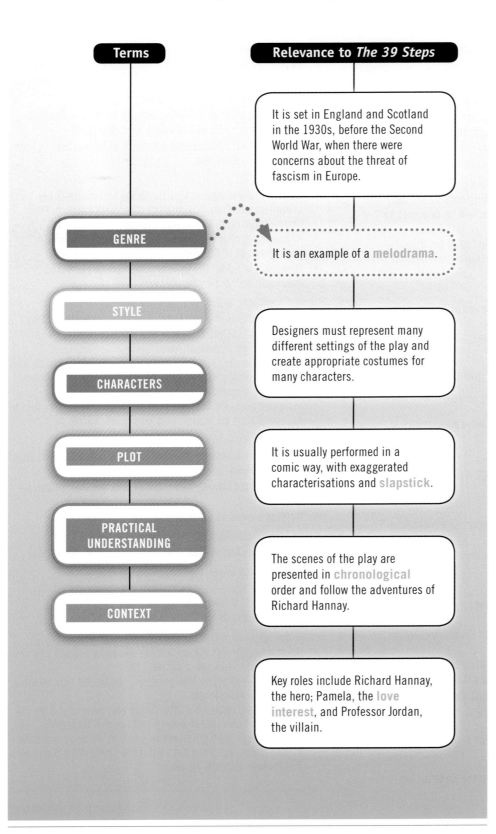

Terms	Relevance to *The 39 Steps*
	It is set in England and Scotland in the 1930s, before the Second World War, when there were concerns about the threat of fascism in Europe.
GENRE	It is an example of a melodrama.
STYLE	Designers must represent many different settings of the play and create appropriate costumes for many characters.
CHARACTERS	
PLOT	It is usually performed in a comic way, with exaggerated characterisations and slapstick.
PRACTICAL UNDERSTANDING	The scenes of the play are presented in chronological order and follow the adventures of Richard Hannay.
CONTEXT	
	Key roles include Richard Hannay, the hero; Pamela, the love interest, and Professor Jordan, the villain.

KEY TERMS

Melodrama: A type of drama with exaggerated characters and exciting events.

Slapstick: Broad physical comedy, including chase scenes and exaggerated fights and tumbles.

Chronological: Events presented in the order in which they occurred.

Love interest: A character's whose primary purpose is their romantic relationship with a central character.

 TIP

As you study the play, make a note of the design challenges, particularly scene changes, including locations in London and Scotland and indoors and outdoors, as well as the varying moods, from comic to romantic to exciting.

Plot: the sequence of the play's main events

ACT 1

▶ *Scene 1: Hannay's Apartment. London. August 1935*
  A restless Richard Hannay decides to go to the theatre.

▶ *Scene 2: Cockney Music Hall. London*
  - Hannay watches a 'Mr. Memory' show at a theatre.
  - A beautiful woman, Annabella Schmidt, sits next to him.
  - Annabella takes out a gun and shoots into the air.
  - Annabella asks Hannay to take her home with him.

▶ *Scene 3: Hannay's Flat. Night*
  - Annabella informs Hannay that she is being pursued by a secret agent and that two men are waiting outside his flat.
  - She explains that top-secret information will be delivered to a foreign country.
  - She warns Hannay of a man missing the top of his little finger and says she must visit an Englishman who lives at Alt-na-Shellach in Scotland.

▶ *Scene 4: Hannay's Flat. Very Late*
  - Annabella dies in Hannay's flat; her last words being 'Alt-na-Shellach.'
  - Hannay covers her body and grabs a map.

▶ *Scene 5: Lobby. Morning*
  - Hannay borrows a cap and coat from a milkman in order to escape the two waiting men.

▶ *Scene 6: Hannay's Flat. Morning*
  - Mrs Higgins, Hannay's charlady, discovers Annabella's body.

▶ *Scene 7: Edinburgh Train. Day*
  - Hannay travels on the train to Edinburgh with two underwear salesmen.

▶ *Scene 8: Edinburgh Station. Day*
  - Salesman 2 reads out the newspaper report of a murder in Hannay's flat.
  - A policeman asks the salesmen to keep their eyes peeled for anything suspicious.

▶ *Scene 9: Highland Train. Day*
  - The police are searching the train for Hannay, who is suspected of Annabella's murder.
  - To escape the police, Hannay bursts into Pamela's carriage and kisses her.
  - When the police leave, Hannay asks Pamela to help him.
  - The policemen return and Pamela reveals Hannay.
  - Hannay leaps out and inches along the outside of the train.
  - A policeman pulls the communication cord, but Hannay flies out of their grasp.

▶ *Scene 10: Forth Bridge. Night*
  - Hannay is hanging onto the bridge.
  - When the police approach, he drops into the water below.

▶ *Scene 11: On the Moors*
  - As Hannay runs across the moors, a radio announcer is heard describing him.

▶ *Scene 12: Crofter's Cottage. Outside*
  - Hannay approaches a Crofter, looking for Alt-na-Shellach.
  - The Crofter introduces his young wife, Margaret.
  - He insists that Hannay stay the night at the cottage in order to get money from him.

▶ *Scene 13: Crofter's Cottage*
  - While the shy Margaret lays the table, Hannay tells her about London. They look at each other with longing. The Crofter interrupts their conversation.
  - Hannay sees that the Crofter has a newspaper with his photograph in it. Margaret notices the photograph.
  - Through a window, the Crofter spies on Margaret and Hannay in earnest conversation.

▶ *Scene 14: Crofter's Cottage. Midnight*
  - Margaret wakes Hannay to tell him the police are coming.
  - The Crofter catches Margaret and Hannay together and accuses them of making love.
  - Hannay tells the Crofter he is on the run from the police and gives him money to hide him. The Crofter takes the money but double-crosses Hannay.
  - Margaret gives Hannay her husband's coat and helps him to escape. Before he leaves, they kiss passionately.

▶ *Scene 15: Scottish Moors. Dawn*
  - Hannay runs across the moors, chased by policemen and dogs.
  - A radio announcer describes the pursuit.
  - Two pilots spot Hannay and shoot at him, but their plane crashes.
  - Hannay arrives at the door of Alt-na-Shellach.

▶ *Scene 16: Alt-na-Shellach*
  - Hannay tells Mrs Jordan that he is a friend of Annabella.

▶ *Scene 17: Alt-na-Shellach. Interior*
  - Mrs Jordan leads Hannay through the house, including showing him the party going on.
  - She leaves him in the study to await the Professor.

▶ *Scene 18: The Professor's Study*
  - Hannay tells the Professor about Annabella's death and that she wanted to tell him a secret.
  - Hannay says that the foreign agent she feared was missing the top of a little finger.
  - The Professor shows his little finger and pulls a gun on Hannay, but Mrs Jordan enters and takes it from him.
  - The Professor invites Hannay to join him. Hannay pretends to consider it, but then asks what the Thirty-Nine Steps are.
  - The Professor shoots Hannay.

KEY TERM

Charlady: A cleaning woman.

ACT 2

▶ *Scene 19: Sheriff's Office*
- Hannay has told the Sheriff that a hymn-book in his pocket kept the bullet from killing him. He urges the Sheriff to apprehend the Professor.
- When a Chief Inspector arrives, the Sheriff and he arrest Hannay for murder, but he escapes.

▶ *Scene 20: City Streets*
- Chased through the city, Hannay hears a marching band and escapes by joining in with them.

▶ *Scene 21: Assembly Hall*
- At a political meeting, Dunwoody and McQuarrie mistake Hanny for their important guest speaker.
- He begins to make a speech to the assembled crowd.
- Pamela enters and, recognising Hannay, rushes out.
- Hannay delivers a rousing speech to wild applause.
- Pamela identifies Hannay to the Inspector.
- Two 'heavies' catch him when he tries to escape.

▶ *Scene 22: Assembly Hall. Foyer*
- Hannay tries to tell Pamela about the foreign agent.
- The Heavies insist that Pamela gets in the car with them all.

▶ *Scene 23: Police Car. Night*
- Pamela questions the route and the car suddenly stops.

▶ *Scene 24: Police Car/Moor*
- A flock of sheep blocks the car and a thick fog descends.
- Pamela and Hannay are handcuffed together.
- Hannay jumps from the car and pulls Pamela along with him, as the Heavies give chase.

▶ *Scene 25: The Dark Moors*
- Hannay and Pamela, still handcuffed and with Hannay pretending he has a gun to keep her quiet, cross the moors.
- They bicker as they become stuck crossing a stile.

▶ *Scene 26: McGarrigle Hotel*
- Claiming to be married, Hannay and Pamela get a room.

▶ *Scene 27: Hotel Bedroom*
- Mrs McGarrigle brings supper to Hannay and Pamela.
- With difficulty, as still handcuffed, Pamela removes some of her wet clothing.
- Hannay falls asleep.
- Pamela manages to ease off the handcuff and leaves.

▶ *Scene 28: Hotel Lobby. Night*
- Pamela overhears the Heavies admitting that they are not the real police.
- They say that the Professor is heading to the London Palladium and then leaving the country.
- They ask the McGarrigles if they have a young couple staying with them. The McGarrigles deny that they do and tell the Heavies to leave.

▶ *Scene 29: Hotel Bedroom*
- Pamela tells Hannay that she knows he was telling the truth and that the Heavies are heading for the London Palladium.
- Hannay and Pamela argue because she didn't tell him sooner, and Hannay exits.

▶ *Scene 30: London Palladium Stage*
- Hannay is joined in the audience by Pamela. He spots the Professor in a box seat.
- Pamela tells Hannay she has been to Scotland Yard to tell her uncle about the plot.
- The 'Mr Memory' show begins and Hannay realises that the secret information is in Mr Memory's memory.
- Chief Inspector Albright arrives to arrest Hannay for murder.
- Hannay escapes and asks Mr Memory what the Thirty-Nine Steps are. Mr Memory begins to reveal that the Thirty-Nine Steps is an organisation of spies.
- The Professor shoots Mr Memory and threatens Pamela.
- The Professor and Hannay wrestle for the gun. The Professor is shot and killed.

▶ *Scene 31: London Palladium. Backstage*
- The dying Mr Memory gives details of the new engine that he had memorised.

▶ *Scene 32: Outside Palladium. Night*
- Pamela tells Hannay he is a free man and they part.

▶ *Scene 33: Hannay's Flat. Night*
- Pamela arrives in Hannay's flat, declaring, 'This is the man I want, Inspector.'
- They kiss before a Christmas tree as snow falls at the window.

Task B1

Explain three ways in which you could show the differences between interior and exterior scenes. Consider changes in:

- Lighting
- Sound
- Performance
- Costumes
- Set.

Provide specific examples of each specialism.

💡 **TIP**

You will not be asked just to describe the plot of the play. You must show an understanding of the play as a whole and how events affect characterisation and design.

⏱ **CHECK IT OUT**

For a full synopsis of the play, see pages 74–75 of *AQA GCSE Drama.*

John Serembe as McQuarrie, Harlequin Productions ▲

When did it happen?

Task B2

Below are 12 key plot points from *The 39 Steps*. Put them in the the order in which they occur in the play, numbering them 1 to 12.

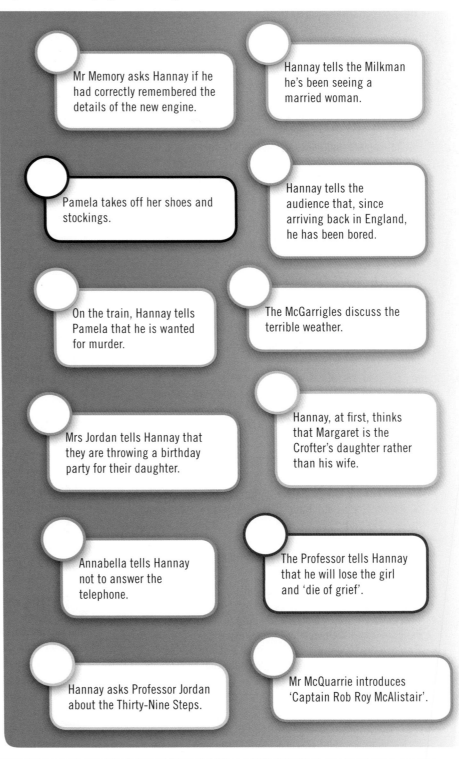

Mr Memory asks Hannay if he had correctly remembered the details of the new engine.

Hannay tells the Milkman he's been seeing a married woman.

Pamela takes off her shoes and stockings.

Hannay tells the audience that, since arriving back in England, he has been bored.

On the train, Hannay tells Pamela that he is wanted for murder.

The McGarrigles discuss the terrible weather.

Mrs Jordan tells Hannay that they are throwing a birthday party for their daughter.

Hannay, at first, thinks that Margaret is the Crofter's daughter rather than his wife.

Annabella tells Hannay not to answer the telephone.

The Professor tells Hannay that he will lose the girl and 'die of grief'.

Hannay asks Professor Jordan about the Thirty-Nine Steps.

Mr McQuarrie introduces 'Captain Rob Roy McAlistair'.

Task B3

In your opinion, when is the play's climax?

Write three sentences to explain your choice.

KEY TERM

Climax: The moment of highest tension in a play, usually of great importance, and often the culmination of earlier events.

Who said that?

 TEST YOURSELF B2

Based on your reading of the play and your understanding of the main characters, match the line of dialogue with the correct character.

See if you can remember too in which scene each line is spoken.

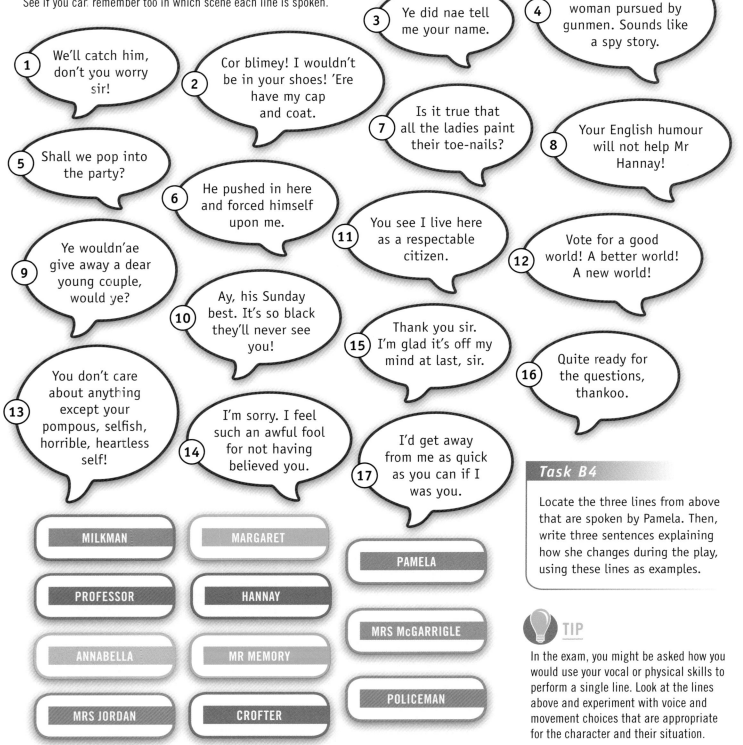

1 We'll catch him, don't you worry sir!

2 Cor blimey! I wouldn't be in your shoes! 'Ere have my cap and coat.

3 Ye did nae tell me your name.

4 Beautiful mysterious woman pursued by gunmen. Sounds like a spy story.

5 Shall we pop into the party?

6 He pushed in here and forced himself upon me.

7 Is it true that all the ladies paint their toe-nails?

8 Your English humour will not help Mr Hannay!

9 Ye wouldn'ae give away a dear young couple, would ye?

10 Ay, his Sunday best. It's so black they'll never see you!

11 You see I live here as a respectable citizen.

12 Vote for a good world! A better world! A new world!

13 You don't care about anything except your pompous, selfish, horrible, heartless self!

14 I'm sorry. I feel such an awful fool for not having believed you.

15 Thank you sir. I'm glad it's off my mind at last, sir.

16 Quite ready for the questions, thankoo.

17 I'd get away from me as quick as you can if I was you.

MILKMAN   MARGARET

PROFESSOR   HANNAY

ANNABELLA   MR MEMORY

MRS JORDAN   CROFTER

PAMELA

MRS McGARRIGLE

POLICEMAN

Task B4

Locate the three lines from above that are spoken by Pamela. Then, write three sentences explaining how she changes during the play, using these lines as examples.

TIP

In the exam, you might be asked how you would use your vocal or physical skills to perform a single line. Look at the lines above and experiment with voice and movement choices that are appropriate for the character and their situation.

Key characters

You will need to demonstrate that you understand the characters in the play, including the different ways they could be characterised and performed. Although *The 39 Steps* has many characters, it is written so that it can be peformed by just four actors. One plays Richard Hannay, and the other three actors **multi-role**.

The descriptions below summarise the main characters.

One character played by one actor

RICHARD HANNAY

- Thirty-seven-year-old bachelor.
- 'Attractive', 'sound in wind and limb'.
- Resourceful and adventurous.
- The play's **protagonist**.

Three characters usually played by one actor

ANNABELLA SCHMIDT

- An exotic German secret agent.
- 'Beautiful and nervous'.
- There is romantic tension between her and Hannay.
- Her death is a **catalyst** for the play's actions.

MARGARET

- The Crofter's wife.
- An 'incredibly pretty Scottish girl'.
- Shy and attracted to Hannay.
- Helps Hannay to escape.

PAMELA

- A train passenger.
- 'Breathtakingly beautiful'.
- The progress of her and Hannay's relationship is a **subplot** to the main secret agent plot.
- She is the play's love interest.

Several characters played by two 'Clown' actors

MR MEMORY

- A performer in a London theatre.
- Uses his remarkable memory to answers questions from the audience.
- This skill forms part of the play's **resolution**, as he knows the secret of the Thirty-Nine Steps.

MILKMAN

- A working-class Londoner.
- Speaks in Cockney dialect: 'Cor blimey', 'whatchoo', 'perfick'.
- Tricked by Hannay into helping him escape.

COMPERE

- Part of a comic partnership with Mr Memory.
- Introduces and supports his act.

KEY TERMS

Multi-role: One actor playing more than one character (multiple roles).

Protagonist: The leading character.

Catalyst: Something or someone who starts a reaction or triggers events

Subplot: A secondary storyline, less important than the main plot.

Resolution: The point at which most plot elements have been settled.

Double act: Two performers who work closely together.

Antagonist: A character who opposes, works against or brings down the protagonist.

Trilby: A soft, narrow-brimmed felt hat.

Trench coat: A belted raincoat, usually in beige or tan.

Comic relief: Light-hearted characters or interludes that provide a break from more intense, serious sections of a drama.

Intonation: The rise and fall of pitch in the voice; the musicality of speech.

CROFTER

- 'An ancient and surly Scottish crofter' (farmer).
- Married to a much younger woman.
- Suspicious of Hannay.
- Despite taking a bribe from Hannay, he still informs on him.

MRS JORDAN

- 'A severe-looking grey-haired lady in tweeds'.
- Married to Professor Jordan.
- Involved in her husband's activities and is heard complaining to the Heavies on the phone.
- When she believes Hannay is dead, she joins her husband in a wild dance.

SHERIFF

- An apparently jovial Scottish sheriff.
- He reveals himself to be loyal to the Professor and turns on Hannay.
- He tries to have Hannay arrested for murder, but Hannay escapes.

PROFESSOR JORDAN

- At first appears to be a wealthy English professor.
- Revealed to be a German agent.
- Tries to recruit Hannay to his cause, and, when he fails, he tries to kill Hannay.
- When he is killed, it contributes to the play's final resolution.
- He is the antagonist or villain of the play.

SALESMAN 1 AND 2

- 'Garrulous' (talkative) underwear salesmen.
- They form a comic double act.
- Their light-hearted dialogue contrasts with Hannay's tense situation.

MR AND MRS McGARRIGLE

- A Scottish couple who run a hotel.
- Mrs McGarrigle is a romantic who enjoys encouraging 'young doves' like Hannay and Pamela.
- They refuse to tell the Heavies about the 'dear young couple'.

HEAVY 1 AND 2

- Two henchmen of the Professor who pretend to be police officers.
- They wear 'trilbies and trench coats'.
- Another double-act, but suggesting more threat of violence than the others.

DUNWOODY AND McQUARRIE

- They are setting up a political meeting.
- Dunwoody is the Master of Ceremonies.
- McQuarrie is the Chairman.
- Dunwood is 'fussy and doddery'.
- McQuarrie is 'even more ancient and doddery'.
- The 'two old men' provide comic relief through their mistake over Hannay's identity.

Task B5

Study the list of characters that the two 'Clown' actors are required to play. Choose three and explain how the actors could make them distinctive and immediately recognisable. Consider:

- Body language
- Posture
- Accent
- Facial expression
- Intonation
- Use of gesture.

 TIP

As you experiment with portraying the characters in Task B5, think about how their occupations and locations could affect the physical or vocal choices that actors might make when performing them.

The 39 Steps in context

The context of a play includes the wider events, circumstances and influences of the period represented in the play:

▶ Social

▶ Historical

▶ Political.

The characters in the play are affected by where they live, as well as the politics, economics and concerns of the time.

You will be expected to demonstrate how you could use the context of the play to influence design choices. An understanding of the context will also provide insight into the play's themes and the characters' feelings and motivations.

The play *The 39 Steps* was inspired both by the novel by John Buchan and the popular 1935 film of it, directed by Alfred Hitchcock, but is also an affectionate parody of period action thrillers. Set in the 1930s, the play emphasises this historic context by the way characters speak and behave, as well as its presentation of the distinctive locations of London and Scotland.

KEY TERMS

Parody: An exaggerated, but sometimes affectionate, imitation made for comic effect.

Thrillers: Books, plays or films that create excitement and suspense with plots that usually revolve around crime and deception.

Fascism: A dictatorial form of government with extreme, intolerant views and practices.

Affluent: Wealthy, prosperous, well off.

Advertisements in Picadilly Circus, c.1935 ▼

Historical background

▶ The play is set in August 1935, before the start of the Second World War.

▶ Adolf Hitler became Chancellor of Germany in 1933 and radically changed how the country was ruled. With this change in leadership, much of Europe feared the rise of fascism.

▶ In the play, Annabella and Professor Jordan are both German, but are working on different political sides.

▶ When Professor Jordan refers to the 'master race' (page 40), he is echoing a common phrase used in Nazi speech which idealised the purity of the Aryan race.

▶ Annabella supports 'Demokratikisch' (page 41) – democracy – and, given who is ruling in Germany at this time, feels that she has 'no country' (page 8).

▶ Hannay refers to the 'rumours of war' (page 2) that are dominating the newspapers. Newspapers and the radio were primary sources of information about current events at the time.

▶ Hannay is portrayed as a patriotic figure who is willing to risk his life to save his country.

▶ In 1939, when the Second World War began, Britain and its allies were fighting Germany.

1930s society: employment, education and entertainment

▶ Hannay is presented as being a relatively affluent character: he belongs to a gentleman's club, goes out regularly and employs a cleaning woman.

▶ He lives in rented accommodation in central London and stresses his unsettled, bachelor lifestyle, while many of his friends are settling down to steady jobs and marriages, or have succumbed to the dangers of their adventurous lives.

▶ In the 1930s, there were chances for employment and education for women, with roughly one-third of women in Britain working outside the home.

▶ The opportunities for women at this time are shown by Annabella and Pamela, who are assured, independent-minded, single women. This contrasts with the isolated and dependent, unhappily married Margaret.

▶ London is depicted as a lively city in which there are many diversions, which contrasts with the isolated Crofter's cottage.

▶ Sexual relationships outside marriage were frowned on by society. Respectable hotels were expected to check that a couple was married before allowing them to share a room.

Culture: film and fashion

▶ Popular entertainment included radio programmes, gramophones (record players), the cinema and the theatre. Jazz music, largely imported from America, was popular, as were show tunes from musicals.

▶ Fashions were often influenced by images from magazines or the clothing of movie stars. Women's fashions were more modest in length and marked the return of a more fitted silhouette compared with the 1920s. Skirts were usually mid-calf length and the waistline was often cinched in and belted.

▶ Thrillers were a popular genre of film in the 1930s. Alfred Hitchcock, the English director

Michael Redgrave and Margaret Lockwood in The Lady Vanishes ▲

of the film version of *The 39 Steps*, was considered a master of this genre. The play of *The 39 Steps* replicates some aspects of the film, while exaggerating and parodying others. Other famous thrillers directed by Hitchcock include *The Man Who Knew Too Much* (1934) and *The Lady Vanishes* (1938.)

▶ The 1930s were also a golden age for mystery and crime novels, including those of the popular English author Agatha Christie. Christie's work was known for its fast pace, snappy dialogue and clever plotting, where, in the last pages, all the pieces of the puzzle would fall into place.

The theme of disguise

Task B6

1 Locate at least three incidents in the play in which a character disguises who or what they really are.

2 For each of your chosen incidents, describe how the deception might be achieved on stage through performance and/or design.

3 Write a short paragraph to explain how the use of disguise suits the play's genre and message.

KEY TERMS

Musical: A type of play in which music, singing and dancing play a significant part.

Silhouette: The outline or shape of a figure.

Pace: The speed or rate at which something happens.

 TIP

In the exam, you will be writing about the context of *The 39 Steps*, which is Britain in the 1930s. You will need to have practical design ideas that show your understanding of this context.

 **CHECK IT OUT**

For more information about the context of *The 39 Steps*, and more photographs, go to pages 75–76 in *AQA GCSE Drama*.

 **TEST YOURSELF B3**

From your understanding of the play and the contexts described here, answer the following questions:

1 What year does the play take place?

2 How is the German background of Annabella shown in the play?

3 What kind of music is playing at the Jordans' party?

4 By what means do characters learn that Hannay is a wanted man?

5 What are some examples of period clothing mentioned in the play?

6 How do the politics of the time influence the plot?

Costumes that reflect context

Costumes are an important design element in a drama production. They influence the audience's perception of the characters, the time period and the physical setting.

If asked about costumes in Question 1 of the exam, you will need to offer design ideas that show evidence of the context of play, which is Britain in the 1930s.

When designing a costume, you might consider:

▶ Style, cut and fit
▶ Colour, fabric, decorative features (buttons, trim, ribbons and so on)
▶ Condition (worn or new, neat or wrinkled, clean or stained and so on)
▶ Footwear
▶ Headgear
▶ Accessories
▶ Make-up and hairstyle.

When creating these, you need to bear in mind the **status**, occupation and social role of the character. These will influence how the character looks, and they are also attributes of the character that you need to be able to put across to the audience.

Fashions

After the styles of the 1920s, which were notable for women wearing short, low-waisted dresses, with a boyish silhouette and cutting their hair short, the 1930s marked a movement to more traditional and mature clothing. Dresses were usually mid-calf length and suggested a V-shape with broader shoulders and slim waist and hips. Fabric was often **bias-cut**, which created a draping and clinging effect and produced a slinky silhouette. Women grew their hair longer and curled it.

After the First World War, many women had retained their roles in the workplace and their clothing styles reflected their responsible jobs, such as tailored jackets or skirt suits. Blouses, however, were often highly feminine, with bows or other decorative details at the collars. Evening wear for this period followed the trend for smooth, sleek shapes and fabrics and was associated with elegance, glamour and sophistication.

The silhouette for men's clothing tended to emphasise their strength, with broad shoulders, slim waists and tapered legs. The width of the male chest was highlighted by the frequent use of **double-breasted** jackets or coats. Men and women would both usually wear a hat when outside.

The outfits that characters would wear would be influenced by the amount of money they had to spend, their occupations and their concern with what was fashionable.

> ### KEY TERMS
>
> **Status:** The social or professional standing of a person.
>
> **Bias-cut:** A tailoring technique where fabric is cut on the diagonal rather than straight across.
>
> **Double-breasted:** A coat or jacket with two lines of buttons down the front rather than one.

Costumes for male characters

Jackets
- Wool, patterns such as herringbone, tweed (including Harris tweed), checked or striped.
- Pads to emphasise shoulders, then tapering to the waist.

Shirts
Long sleeved, button-down collars, usually white.

Trousers
High-waisted, with a pleat from the waist in the centre of each leg.

Colours
Often subtle and muted, such as navy blue, browns and greys.

Evening wear
- Velvet smoking jacket with shawl collar.
- White jacket.
- Tuxedo suit.

Accessories
- Pocket handkerchief in front jacket pocket.
- Brightly coloured or patterned ties or cravats for daywear; bow tie/dicky bow for evening wear.

Jumpers
Often associated with the working class, as a practical way of keeping warm for outdoor work, or as an item of sportswear. Frequently, these knitted garments were home-made.

Suits
Matching jackets and trousers. Three-piece suits that included a matching waistcoat were popular.

Coats
- Woollen double-breasted top coat, mid-calf length.
- Trench coat: a longer waterproof coat with a belt.

Hats
- Working class: flat caps.
- Business and formal hats: trilbies, fedoras, bowlers or top hats.

Footwear
- Brogues or two-toned Oxfords.
- Leather, usually in a colour to match the clothing.
- Patterned socks.

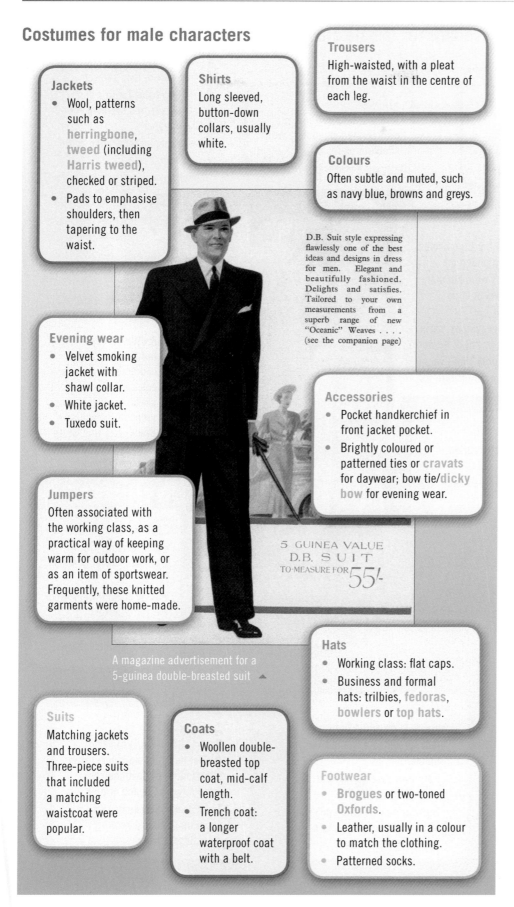

D.B. Suit style expressing flawlessly one of the best ideas and designs in dress for men. Elegant and beautifully fashioned. Delights and satisfies. Tailored to your own measurements from a superb range of new "Oceanic" Weaves . . . . (see the companion page)

5 GUINEA VALUE
D.B. SUIT
TO·MEASURE FOR 55/-

A magazine advertisement for a 5-guinea double-breasted suit ▲

KEY TERMS

Herringbone: A pattern made up of rows of 'v' shapes.

Tweed: A thick wool fabric consisting of more than one colour.

Harris tweed: An exclusive, high-quality, handwoven, woollen cloth.

Dicky bow: An informal term for a bow tie, which is a type of neck tie shaped into a bow, usually worn on formal occasions.

Cravat: A piece of fabric, wider than a tie, usually in a bold colour or pattern and typically worn tucked into an open-necked shirt collar.

Fedora: A hat that resembles a trilby, but with a wider brim.

Bowler: A black hat with a rounded top and a small brim, often associated with the English 'city gent'.

Top hat: A formal hat, usually in a smooth black fabric, which has a tall, cylindrical shape and a brim.

Brogues: Laced shoes with ornamental perforated patterns.

Oxfords: Plain, formal, lace-up shoes.

 TIP

The condition of the characters' costumes might indicate the nature of their work. For example, the condition of the Crofter's coat might be dirty and patched compared with Hannay's clean and pressed Harris tweed coat.

Costumes for female characters

Dress/skirt
- For evening, long, elegant dresses in silk or satin.
- For daywear, dress or skirt, fitted at the waist and mid-calf length.

Jackets
Tailored, wool. Often exaggerated shoulders, with shoulder pads.

Blouses
- Short or long sleeved.
- Expensive fabrics such as silk and satin, or the cheaper.
- Scoop or V neckline, with bows.

Hats
Small caps decorated with feathers or bows, or wide-brimmed felt hats, frequently, **asymmetrical** or worn tilted to one side.

Shoes
- **Kitten heel** or high heeled; pointed or rounded toe.
- T-bar straps were popular, as were bows or other decorations.
- For formal occasions, satin **court shoes** might be worn.
- Boots or sturdy shoes would usually be worn for farming.

Colours
A wide variety, but outfits usually coordinated. Popular colours included: pinks, mauves, grass green and royal blue. Black, grey and white were frequently used for evening wear.

Hair
- Fashions were for chin or shoulder-length; curled or permed.
- In rural areas, hair was often longer and tied back or put up in a simple bun.

Outerwear
- For evening, furs, capes, velvet coats or jackets.
- Day or work wear: wool coats/jackets.
- Rural workers would have woollen shawls.

A page from a ladieswear catalogue, c.1933 ▲

KEY TERMS

Asymmetrical: Having two sides that do not match, or something that leans to one side.

Kitten heel: A shoe with a low, narrow, curved heel, often open at the back, with a strap.

Court shoes: Plain strapless shoes with a raised heel.

Girdle: An undergarment in a stretchy fabric that gives a slim, smooth silhouette to the waist and hips.

Camiknickers: A one-piece undergarment that combines the top of a slip or a camisole with a pair of French knickers.

Make-up
- Lipstick, often in bright reds, provided a defined lipline.
- Eyebrows were strong and shaped into an arch.
- Foundation was pale and often powdered to create a matt effect.

Underwear
- Bra, **girdle**, **camiknickers** (silk or satin for elegance; rayon or cotton for budget choices), often in white, peach or pink.
- Tan coloured stockings, with a seam up the back, kept up with a suspender belt.

Using context to inspire costume design

Study these photographs and think about how they might inspire designs for the female characters in the play.

Draw quick sketches of your ideas.

Remember that the costumes should reflect the play's 1930s context.

TEST YOURSELF B4

Look at the costume items below and select which of these characters the items would suit best:

- Professor Jordan
- The Crofter
- The Heavies.

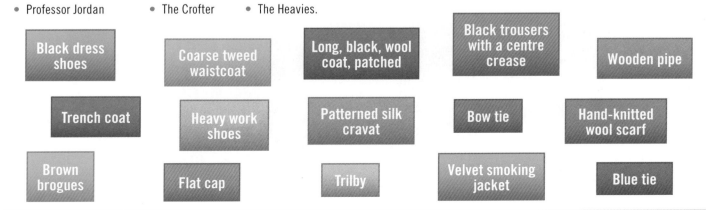

Black dress shoes

Coarse tweed waistcoat

Long, black, wool coat, patched

Black trousers with a centre crease

Wooden pipe

Trench coat

Heavy work shoes

Patterned silk cravat

Bow tie

Hand-knitted wool scarf

Brown brogues

Flat cap

Trilby

Velvet smoking jacket

Blue tie

Uniforms

Several of the characters in the play are identified by their occupations and would wear costumes to suit their jobs.

Study the three photographs below, noticing the details of the outfits.

Then draw three sketches to show your own costume ideas for the Paperboy, the Policemen and the Milkman.

Quick changes

One significant aspect of *The 39 Steps* is that actors sometimes have to undertake quick costume changes when they rapidly swap from one character to another. One way to accomplish this is by having a few distinctive costumes or accessories that can quickly be put on over other clothing.

Task B9

Read page 19 of the script and track all the times the actors change character or costume. Then decide on one distinctive item of clothing or an accessory that each actor could put on to show that they have changed character. The characters that the two 'Clown' actors have to play on this one page are:

- Porter
- Salesman
- Paperboy
- Policeman
- Mrs Higgins.

Transforming costumes

Characters' costumes might change in the course of the play. In *The 39 Steps*, there are a few factors that might cause the designer to add to or alter a character's costume during the play. For example:

▸ Extra items of clothing for warmth or protection, perhaps if a character has just come in or is going out, or if they wear an over garment to keep their clothing clean underneath.

▸ A character might dress with particular care because they are assuming a certain status or making a public appearance, such as a Master of Ceremonies.

▸ If a character is in an unusual situation, such as being awake and out of bed in the middle of the night.

Task B10

Draw sketches of costume ideas for the following moments:
- Mr Memory in Scene 2, page 2
- Mrs Higgins in Scene 6, page 13
- Margaret in Scene 14, page 30.

CHECK IT OUT

Go to the Illuminate website for a free design figure to base your drawings on.

Also look at the costume guidance for Annabella on page 77 of the *AQA GCSE Drama* coursebook.

Make-up and hair

The leading characters in the play would probably wear make-up and hairstyles to replicate the fashions of the 1930s. Men wore their hair short at the back and sides and used a pomade (scented ointment) to style it. A neatly trimmed moustache was fashionable.

Women's make-up frequently emphasised their eyes, with dark liner and mascara, and lips, with bold lipstick. Influenced by film stars of the time, dyed blonde hair was popular.

Task B11

Below is a still showing Madeleine Carroll as Pamela and Robert Donat as Hannay from the 1935 Hitchcock film of *The 39 Steps*. Study it and write about the characters' hair and make-up.

> **KEY TERMS**
>
> Naturalistic: Lifelike, believable, realistic.

Task B12

Draw two sketches showing your hair and make-up ideas for Professor Jordan and Mrs Jordan. Annotate them, explaining how they reflect the 1930s context.

 **CHECK IT OUT**

See page 82 of *AQA GCSE Drama* for more ideas about costuming Professor Jordan.

 **LOOK HERE**

For more ideas about writing about costumes, go to pages 81 and 107–113.

Some characters will not have fashionable make-up or hairstyles. Margaret, less well off and in an isolated situation, might wear her hair either loose or in a plait or bun. Unlike Pamela or Annabella, she would not appear to wear any make-up – as she speaks with wonder at the idea of ladies who 'paint their toe-nails' or 'put rouge and lipsticks on their faces'.

In addition to **naturalistic** hair and make-up choices, you could make some broader design choices if, for example, male actors portray Mrs Higgins, Mrs Jordan or Mrs McGarrigle, or if some characters – such as the Crofter or Mr McGarrigle – have beards. In these cases, wigs or false beards can aid quick transformations.

How the play's context might be shown in set and prop design

Another specialism you might be asked to refer to when discussing the context of a particular extract is the set, which could include stage furnishings and props.

Your ideas will need to take into account the 1930s context of the play.

Set design

When designing a set, you might consider:

- Staging configuration (proscenium, in the round and so on)
- A composite set or a completely different set for each scene
- The scale (how large) your set will be
- Any levels, ramps or stairs
- Locations of the actors' entrances and exits
- Any backdrops, flats or projections
- The colours, textures and shapes used
- Any necessary props or set dressings or furnishings.

A particular challenge of *The 39 Steps* is the number and variety of locations that a designer needs to represent, ranging from a London bachelor's flat to a grand house in Scotland; a West End theatre to a Crofter's cottage. There are also a train, a car and a journey across the moors that need to be conveyed.

1930s architecture and interior design

The sets for Hannay's flat and Alt-na-Shellach might be influenced by the popular Art Deco styles of the time. Art Deco was a distinctive arts and design movement that can be seen in architecture, furniture, art and household items of the time. It was considered modern and fashionable and used up-to-date manufacturing techniques. Art Deco pieces often contained geometric designs and smooth, polished surfaces.

A restored croft in the Outer Hebrides of Scotland ▲

> **KEY TERMS**
>
> **Composite set:** A single set which represents several locations at once.
>
> **Set dressings:** Items on the set not used as props, but which create detail and interest in it, such as a vase, cushions or paintings.

Task B13

Study the examples of Art Deco interior designs below. Then sketch a design for a prop, item of stage furniture or whole set for *The 39 Steps* inspired by these photographs.

Task B14

Make a list of set ideas that will show how different the Crofter's Cottage is compared with Hannay's flat in London.

Crofter's Cottage

A croft is a small area of farm land in Scotland. A crofter's cottage is usually a basic stone structure with a thatched or turfed roof and a chimney. Crofts were usually in isolated, rural locations with few modern conveniences. The script describes the Crofter's cottage as 'miserable'.

Transportation

There are several modes of transport in the play, but, practically, you will not be able to have full replicas of any of these. You might, however, suggest them in their 1930s context through simple but effective means such as the choice of fabrics, shapes and, perhaps, signs with period lettering.

Set design ideas for key scenes

Taking into account the many locations of the play, you need to think about how you can create a practical set that can quickly be changed to represent new settings. You might be able to use just a few key pieces, such a chair and a lamp, or you might choose to use movable flats or projections to create the new locations.

CHECK IT OUT

Go to page 78 of *AQA GCSE Drama* for more detailed guidance on set design.

Task B16

Locate at least one mention of each of these key props and then write two sentences or draw a sketch to show how you think it should look.

- The telephone in Hannay's flat
- Salesman 2's samples case
- Professor Jordan's gun
- Mrs McGarrigle's tray of food.

Task B15

Use the chart below to note your ideas for some of the key locations, including how they will reflect the 1930s and how they could practically be achieved.

Location and basic requirements	Set and prop ideas
Hannay's flat: Armchair, lamp, table, bottle of Scotch, glass, telephone, window, blinds.	
Cockney Music Hall: Stage area, theatre box with at least two seats.	
Edinburgh train: Seats and window in the compartment; exterior.	
Crofter's cottage: Armchair, table, three chairs, window.	
Alt-na-Shellach: Door; Professor's study, including armchair.	

Props

The many props used in the play are another area in which you can establish its period, as well as giving insight into the characters and location.

How lighting and sound contribute to context

Other design specialisms that you might be asked to discuss in relation to the play's context include lighting and sound.

Lighting

When creating a lighting design, you might think about:

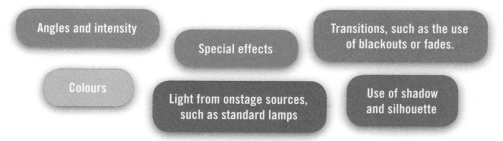

- Angles and intensity
- Special effects
- Transitions, such as the use of blackouts or fades.
- Colours
- Light from onstage sources, such as standard lamps
- Use of shadow and silhouette

In order to suggest the context of *The 39 Steps*, you might use lighting to:

▸ Suggest the time of day, as there are scenes set specifically in the morning, for example, including Scenes 5 and 29, and others where it is important that they take place at night, such as Scene 14 or Scene 23

▸ Show the types of lighting used in the 1930s, such as streetlamps or an electric standard lamp

▸ Indicate the location of the scenes (the lighting at the theatre where Mr Memory performs would be very different from the lighting in a train, for example)

▸ Create atmosphere or the mood of a scene in relation to the play's action or themes, such as the dark moors or the Jordans' party.

Task B17

1 Read Scene 17 and make notes on any moments that stand out as being suitable for a particular lighting design.

2 Consider how you could use lighting to achieve the following:
   - The transition from the previous scene to emphasise the contrast
   - The luxuriousness of Alt-na-Shellach
   - The atmosphere of the party.

3 Read this opening sentence of a sample response about using lighting to suggest the context of the scene. Then, either using this opening or one of your own, complete a paragraph about how lighting could support the action of the scene and show the play's context.

> I want to show how Alt-na-Shellach is a very attractive location, but also a strange one, with danger lurking just around the corner...

CHECK IT OUT

For more information about lighting, look at pages 236–239 in the *AQA GCSE Drama* coursebook.

Task B18

Look at these four student-style answers and identify:

- Where in *The 39 Steps* the lighting idea might be effective
- How it demonstrates the context of the play.

An example has been given to start you off.

To capture the atmosphere of 1930s London, I would use lighting upstage of Hannay's window. A yellow gel in a profile lantern would create the glow of a street light, angled diagonally into the window. To recreate a fog and to add mystery, I would connect a tiny fogger to the lighting rig so that the street lighting is misty. I would also place, upstage, a flashing blue neon sign advertising a Portland Place hotel.

Scene 1: Context: In an urban location such as London in the 1930s, there would be a variety of outside lights, including street lamps and signs. London fog was famous during this period and adds to the sense of danger and mystery.

I will use a low fog machine to create a swirling mist around Hannay's ankles as he tries to escape. Fresnel lanterns placed low on a lighting rig in the wings will shine through this mist. A high-angle profile lantern will project a low-intensity pearly white light to suggest moonlight on a stage which is otherwise very dark. The two Policemen will use torches to search for Hannay. The colour palette of dark greens will reinforce the sense that they are outside at night.

I will use three different followspots for this scene. One will capture Mr Memory on stage; another will be on Hannay and Pamela in their seats; and the third will pick out Professor Jordan in his box. All will be high intensity, with different-coloured filters: a rosy one on Mr Memory; blue for Hannay and Pamela; and an unpleasant green on the Professor. In addition, footlights along the downstage edge will throw ominous shadows onto Mr Memory's face.

I will use a backlight behind a shadow puppet of a small plane. This will be positioned high upstage. A strobe will reinforce the gunfire. Before the plane crashes, I will use a gobo to project onto the stage floor the effect of rapidly spinning swirls, to suggest the plane is out of control. This will be followed by a bright, high-intensity flash to signify the crash.

KEY TERMS

Fogger: A device that produces a smoke that gives the effect of fog or mist.

Colour palette: The range of colours used. For example, a scene might use light colours, dark colours, muted tones, grey tones, earth tones or vivid, primary colours.

Strobe: A lighting device that produces short bursts of light.

Gobo: A metal cut-out used to project patterns, such as leaves, stars, swirls or waves.

Sound

When creating a sound design, you might consider:

- Live or recorded sound
- Sound effects or music
- Volume/amplification
- Sources of sound and the direction of sound.

 **CHECK IT OUT**

See pages 240–243 of *AQA GCSE Drama* to learn more about sound, including advice from a sound designer.

Task B19

Here are some effects a sound designer wants to achieve. How could they create these effects to reflect the context of *The 39 Steps*? An example has been suggested to start you off.

> I want to highlight the immediate attraction between Hannay and Pamela in Scene 9, as well as to mark the sudden change from danger to romance.

> Before Hannay enters Pamela's carriage, I will have recorded noise of a fast-travelling train. One of the Policemen will blow his whistle, with a loud, piercing noise.
>
> When Hannay enters the carriage, a recording of romantic music of the period, such as an instrumental version of 'Isn't It Romantic?', will snap on and become louder when the pair kiss. It will continue until the Policeman enters, when it will suddenly snap off, as if a spell has been broken.

> This is the climax of the play and I want sound design to establish the theatre setting and contribute to the excitement of the scene.

> In Scene 21, I want to show Hannay's growing belief in his speech and how enthusiastically the audience responds to him.

> It is important to contribute to the creation of the car through the use of sound effects, as well as capturing that it is a dangerous night-time location in Scene 23.

Puppet design

Some productions of *The 39 Steps* employ puppets in various scenes. In order to use puppets to reveal the play's context, designs you could consider might include:

- Creating a music hall audience of life-sized puppets for Scene 2
- A small **marionette** of Hannay in 1930s clothing to show his escape from the train and hanging from the Forth Bridge in Scenes 9 and 10
- Shadow puppets of 1930s aeroplanes for Scene 15.

KEY TERM

Marionette: A puppet worked by strings.

 **CHECK IT OUT**

See pages 95 and 253–256 in *AQA GCSE Drama* for more about puppetry, including an interview with a designer.

Shadow puppets designed by Peter McKintosh ◄

Exam-style example question: Component 1, Section B, Question 1

A Focus on Scene 18, The Professor's Study, from 'Voice: Mr Hammond?' to Hannay: I didn't do it!'

You are designing a setting for this extract. The set must reflect the 1930s period setting of *The 39 Steps*. Describe your design ideas for the setting. [4 marks]

B Focus on Scene 3, from 'Annabella: Turn it off!' to 'She marches to the drinks cabinet.'

You are designing a costume for Annabella to wear in a performance of this extract. The costume must reflect the 1930s period setting of *The 39 Steps*. Describe your design ideas for the costume. [4 marks]

C Focus on Scene 29, from the beginning of the scene until 'Pamela: Sorry.'

You are creating a lighting design for this extract. The lighting must reflect the 1930s period of the play. Describe your lighting design ideas. [4 marks]

D Focus on Scene 8, from the beginning of the scene to 'Salesman: Hello!'

You are designing a prop appropriate for this extract. The prop must reflect the 1930s period setting of the play. Describe your ideas for the prop. [4 marks]

E Focus on Scene 15, from 'A plane appears' to 'The stage fills with smoke.'

You are the sound designer for this extract. Describe your ideas for a sound design, bearing in mind the context of *The 39 Steps* set in the 1930s. [4 marks]

F Focus on Scene 24, from 'Wind. Bleating sheep sounds' to 'They chase the sheep and exit.'

You are a puppet designer for the extract. Describe your ideas for a puppet design, bearing in mind the context of *The 39 Steps* set in the 1930s. [4 marks]

Sample answers for Component 1, Section B, Question 1

Task B20

The following extracts are from responses focusing on Scene 21, the Assembly Hall. Read them through and annotate them for mentions of:

- Context, C
- Precise design detail, D
- Understanding of the play and characters, U.

Costume

In this scene, Hannay will retain some of his previous stylish appearance, but he will be disheveled and, at first, wear the Crofter's old overcoat. Ⓤ As appropriate for the 1930s, Ⓒ I will costume Hannay in high-waisted pleated trousers, a broad-shouldered suit jacket and matching waistcoat, in a conventional brown herringbone tweed. The Crofter's patched, black wool coat will hang loosely. Ⓓ It is when Hannay takes off the rough coat that he is mistaken for the important guest speaker. He will straighten his tie and neaten his hair. As he is giving a political speech, I will have Dunwoody place a large, colourful party rosette on his jacket.

Lighting

I will fade up with a wash of bright golden light across the stage, produced by fresnel lanterns in the wings and fly space. When Dunwoody and McQuarrie are at the lectern, a profile spot with a subtle pink filter will be used to focus attention on them. This will create an old-fashioned theatrical effect to reinforce the period setting.

Set

To create a 1930s Assembly Hall, I will have a large cloth banner with 'Vote McCorquodale' drop down from the fly space, along with metres of brightly coloured bunting, strung stage right to stage left, creating an optimistic, old-fashioned atmosphere. A truck will be used to push on a small wooden stage centre stage with a 1930s microphone on a stand and a lectern. Dunwoody will bring on a stack of period oak folding chairs, placed at either side of the stage.

Sound

I want to capture the mood of ordinary people in Britain in the 1930s. To begin, I will play a recording of a marching band tune, perhaps including bagpipes. This will gradually fade during the opening lines of the scene. I will have a practical, 1930s-style stand microphone on stage to amplify the speakers' voices. Recorded applause will give the impression of an enthusiastic audience. However, to emphasise the artificiality and to create a comic effect, I will have the applause snap on and off.

Props and stage furnishings

Although Art Deco furniture might be seen in fashionable areas, I believe that in this rural location, the Assembly Hall furniture would be more practical. When designing the lectern, I would aim for a sturdy and old-fashioned look, such as heavy oak, with a slanted top, on which speech notes could be put. I would have 'Assembly Hall' etched into the front of it in a traditional serif style. As I want to suggest it has been used for years, it will be distressed.

Characterisation

You need to understand how different roles in the play could be performed. The playwright has given indications about the characters and their backgrounds, feelings and desires. Actors and directors must use their skills to convey these ideas.

Areas to consider when developing a performance include:

▸ The character's importance to the play
▸ Whether the character changes and develops during the play
▸ How an actor could use vocal and physical skills to portray the character
▸ In what ways an actor could use the stage space and interact with others
▸ How the play's context and style might influence acting choices
▸ What the character's thoughts, feelings and motivations are and how these could be put across to the audience or influence acting choices
▸ How the subtext of the character's lines could be expressed
▸ What impact the actor's choices would have on the audience's understanding.

KEY TERMS

Motivations: The feelings behind what a character wants or needs.

Subtext: The unspoken meaning, feelings and thoughts 'beneath' the lines, which might be shown in the characters' body language, tone of voice and facial expressions.

Three big-screen interpretations of Hannay: Kenneth Moore, Robert Powell and Robert Donat ▾ ▸

✓ TEST YOURSELF B5

The following descriptions indicate some of the important features to be considered when developing characterisations.
Match each one with the correct character from *The 39 Steps*.

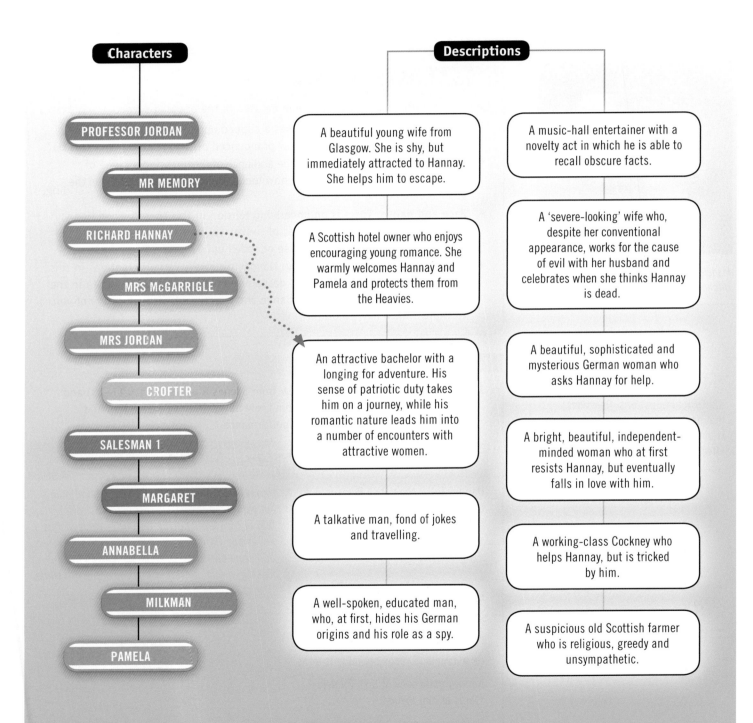

Characters

PROFESSOR JORDAN

MR MEMORY

RICHARD HANNAY

MRS McGARRIGLE

MRS JORDAN

CROFTER

SALESMAN 1

MARGARET

ANNABELLA

MILKMAN

PAMELA

Descriptions

A beautiful young wife from Glasgow. She is shy, but immediately attracted to Hannay. She helps him to escape.

A music-hall entertainer with a novelty act in which he is able to recall obscure facts.

A Scottish hotel owner who enjoys encouraging young romance. She warmly welcomes Hannay and Pamela and protects them from the Heavies.

A 'severe-looking' wife who, despite her conventional appearance, works for the cause of evil with her husband and celebrates when she thinks Hannay is dead.

An attractive bachelor with a longing for adventure. His sense of patriotic duty takes him on a journey, while his romantic nature leads him into a number of encounters with attractive women.

A beautiful, sophisticated and mysterious German woman who asks Hannay for help.

A bright, beautiful, independent-minded woman who at first resists Hannay, but eventually falls in love with him.

A talkative man, fond of jokes and travelling.

A working-class Cockney who helps Hannay, but is tricked by him.

A well-spoken, educated man, who, at first, hides his German origins and his role as a spy.

A suspicious old Scottish farmer who is religious, greedy and unsympathetic.

TIP

The play *The 39 Steps* is heavily influenced by the 1935 Alfred Hitchcock film. In order to understand what the playwright Patrick Barlow is parodying, it is worth watching excerpts from the film. Note how the characters speak and move.

Madeleine Carroll and Robert Donat in Hitchcock's 1935 film ▲

KEY TERM

Rhetorical questions: Questions that do not demand an answer as it is already implied, but are asked for effect or to make a point.

Characterisation focus on Richard Hannay

Hannay is the play's protagonist and the audience is following his journey throughout the play. He is on stage for most of the play, driving the action through his adventurous choices. His character is revealed through his dialogue, actions and what other characters say about him.

We meet Hannay in Scene 1 when he speaks directly to the audience. From his very first words, the audience will be making judgements about him.

Task B21

Experiment with vocal skills that could be used in the opening scene:

- **Accent/dialect:** Hannay usually has a clipped upper-middle-class English accent, typical of 1930s films. How pronounced or exaggerated might this be?
- **Volume:** Hannay is speaking to the audience and expressing a range of emotions. How might that affect how loudly or softly he speaks? Does the volume vary during the speech?
- **Pace and pause:** There is an underlying tension in this speech when Hannay talks of boredom and asks a series of rhetorical questions. Would there be any moments when he might pause or speed up?
- **Intonation and emotional range:** Hannay expresses various emotions in this scene, including anger, boredom, despair and excitement. Locate when in the speech you think his emotions change and experiment with your tone of voice to express each new emotion.

Task B22

1   Look at the stage directions below from Scenes 8 and 9 (pages 17–23) and make notes on what you learn from them about Hannay's thoughts and motivations and possibilities for performance.

Stage directions	Thoughts and motivations to note in performance
Hannay takes the paper. Pores into it. Looks up to see both men staring at him.	*Hanny fears being discovered. His desire to find out what is in the newspaper conflicts with his fear of his identity being revealed by suspicious behaviour. Hannay should quickly grab the paper and stare closely at it. When he notices the men looking at him, he will look guilty and try to smile.*
Hannay freezes.	
Hannay is trapped. Both policemen march towards him.	
He bursts in. Sweeps her into his arms.	
Hannay pulls back at last, Pamela stares at him aghast.	
Policeman 1 leaps after Hannay, who is inching along the outside of the train, hanging onto his hat.	

Continued on next page ▶

2 Look in detail at the stage direction 'Hannay pulls back at last...' on page 22. With a partner, create a **still image** to show the stage relationship between Hannay and Pamela at this point. You might consider:

- Eye contact
- Body language
- Facial expression
- Physical **proximity**.

Then write at least three sentences explaining how the characters of Hannay and Pamela could be demonstrated by the actors' choices for this stage direction.

> **KEY TERMS**
>
> Still image: An acting technique when the actors freeze a moment in silence, showing the characters' positions and facial expressions.
>
> Proximity: How near people or objects are to each other; also referred to as 'proxemics', which describes the relative positions of characters on stage.

Character development

Throughout the play, Richard Hannay's character develops as the plot tests him. He is shown to change from a bored bachelor to an action hero to a happily married man.

Task B23

Use the chart below to note how the actor playing Hannay might use their vocal and physical skills to trace the changes in the character. Some suggestions have been provided, but add your own ideas and interpretation.

Scene	Key events involving Hannay	Acting techniques	Acting choices and effects
1	• Hannay is introduced to the audience and reveals his frustrations with his life. • He decides he must pull himself together and heads off to a West End show.	Vocal skills	• Hannay will use his upper-middle-class English accent and speak in a clipped 1930s manner. • Although his tone is casual and sophisticated early in the speech, it will grow more ragged and emotional, especially when he says 'I could quite easily just –', suggesting that he wishes he was dead. • There will be a complete change of tone when he decides to go to the theatre.
		Physical skills	• He will be casually seated in an armchair with his legs crossed, making eye contact with the audience. • He will stand on 'And I thought' and begin pacing the room. He will grab the glass of Scotch and quickly gulp it down. • When he has his 'brainwave', he will clap his hands.
		Impact on audience	• The audience will understand through his direct address that they are meant to sympathise with him. • They will anticipate that his restlessness will lead him into danger and adventure.
3	• Hannay has brought Annabella back to his flat. • The phone rings and she tells him not to answer it. • She tells him that she must go to Scotland. • She goes into another room, leaving him 'confused and mesmerised'.	Vocal skills	• Hannay's English accent will contrast with Annabella's German one. • He will speak in a lightly teasing way when he makes fun of her story, saying she should be 'more careful' and that it sounds like something from 'a spy story'. • As they are alone at night, he will be quieter than in the previous scene.

Continued on next page ▶

Scene	Key events involving Hannay	Acting techniques	Acting choices and effects
		Physical skills	• The close proximity between the characters will emphasise their attraction. • Hannay will mainly move in an elegant, athletic way, though there are also opportunities for physical comedy, such as when he wrestles with the blind.
		Impact on audience	The audience will sense the 'electricity' between the two characters, but it will be shown in an understated way.
9	• Hannay tries to escape the police. • He uses a kiss with Pamela to 'hide'. • He escapes outside the train.	Vocal skills	
		Physical skills	
		Impact on audience	Hannay is seen as a resourceful action hero who is able to think on his feet and take physical risks.
18	• Hannay meets Professor Jordan and realises the Professor is a secret agent. • He refuses the Professor's offer to join him. • He is shot by Professor Jordan.	Vocal skills	
		Physical skills	
		Impact on audience	The audience realises that Hannay has patriotic beliefs that he will defend even if they lead to his death.
21	Hannay is mistaken for a guest speaker at a campaign rally and delivers a rousing patriotic speech.	Vocal skills	
		Physical skills	
		Impact on audience	• The audience sees how well Hannay can think on his feet, while also expressing his very real ideas about what he values, such as people 'doing the best they can'. • His charisma and enthusiasm are delightful.
33	Hannay and Pamela are happily married.	Vocal skills	
		Physical skills	
		Impact on audience	

 CHECK IT OUT

For more ideas about approaching the character of Hannay, see page 83 of *AQA GCSE Drama*.

Task B24

The happily married man at the end of the play is very different from the despairing bachelor of the first scene. Draw a sketch to represent Hannay in the first scene and then a contrasting one for the last scene. Annotate your sketches to describe:

- Facial expression
- Posture and body language
- Use of gesture
- Positioning on stage.

Characterisation focus on Pamela and Annabella

Typically, Pamela and Annabella would be played by the same actor. Though they are both attractive women, they should be portrayed very differently, including how they speak, move and dress.

Task B25

Look at these adjectives and select three that you think best describe Pamela and three that best describe Annabella.

Mysterious

Angry

Confident

Athletic

Practical

Intelligent

German

Elegant

Suspicious

Determined

Romantic

Brave

Resourceful

Conventional

Frightened

English

Businesslike

Comic

Vocal skills: accents

One of the key differences between Annabella and Pamela will be their accents. Annabella has a German accent, which adds to her sense of mystery and sophistication but is also a source of some comedy in her scenes with Hannay, whereas Pamela will probably speak in a middle-class or upper-middle-class English accent. In addition, Annabella might use her voice in a seductive way in order to get Hannay to do what she wants, whereas Pamela is frequently arguing and bickering with him, so would employ a very different tone.

Olivia Greene as Annabella ▲

 **CHECK IT OUT**

For more notes on Pamela, see pages 84, 85 and 88 of *AQA GCSE Drama*.

Task B26

Experiment with the following lines spoken by Annabella. Then make notes on how you could use your vocal skills to express her character suited to the situation she is in. What effect do you achieve?

> Bleint! Bleint! Pull the bleint! (page 6)
>
> Bring it to my room. (page 10)
>
> Now there is – (*barely audible*) – no turning back! Oh, my dear Richard! (page 11)

Vocal skills: subtext

Your vocal choices for Pamela might be influenced by use of subtext. There are occasions when Pamela is saying one thing but thinking or meaning something else: when she has to be polite and affectionate to Hannay in front of Mrs McGarrigle, for example, or when she is angry with Hannay but also attracted to him.

Task B27

Look at Pamela's lines of dialogue below and decide:
- The subtext – what she is thinking
- What vocal choices you could make to reveal her thoughts.

> Darling! (page 61)
>
> I want you to know I hate you! (page 63)
>
> AND DON'T EXPECT ME TO COME WITH YOU!!!! (page 70)

Annabella and Pamela in relation to Hannay

Both Annabella and Pamela are important to Hannay and what happens to him. Annabella sets him off on his adventure, and Pamela both obstructs and then ultimately aids him on it.

Task B28

Keep in mind the words you have chosen to describe the characters in the previous tasks. Work with a partner to create a still image showing the physical postures and positions of Annabella and Pamela when they first meet Hannay.

Consider:
- What is the proximity of each character to Hannay?
- How might their postures differ?
- What gestures might they use?
- What are their facial expressions like?

Focus on the following scenes:

> Annabella: May I come home with you? (page 5)
>
> *Pamela, who appears before him another compartment…* (page 21)

Physical comedy

This type of comic acting requires inventive uses of the body. It might involve slapstick, exaggerated movement, sudden falls, double-takes and mime.

One particular source of humour is created by the characters' unexpected proximity to Hannay. In Annabella's case, this occurs in Scene 4, when Hannay thinks she has come to kiss him, but instead she dies in his arms. With Pamela, there are many opportunities for physical comedy when she is handcuffed to Hannay.

Task B29

1 Working with a partner, experiment with different ways of using physical skills and the stage space for the following scenes:
   • Annabella's death (Scene 4, page 11)
   • Pamela and Hannay handcuffed at the McGarrigle Hotel (Scene 27, page 62).

2 Write a paragraph for each scene, explaining how your choices would contribute to the audience's understanding of the characters and their situation and the play's comedy.

KEY TERMS

Double-take: To look at something once, then realise what you have seen and immediately look a second time. This comic technique indicates a sense of surprise at what was first seen or the slowness of the mind to believe or understand what has been seen.

Mime: To act without words, or to use movement, gesture and facial expression to create objects or a narrative.

✓ TEST YOURSELF B6

The descriptions below give aspects of the three female characters typically portrayed by one actor. Read each description and decide which of the characters it is appropriate for.

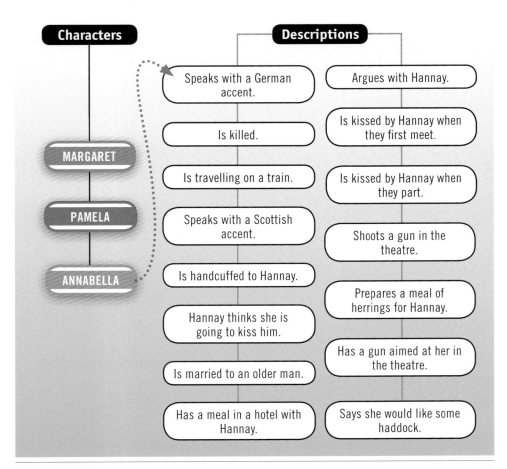

Characters

MARGARET

PAMELA

ANNABELLA

Descriptions

Speaks with a German accent.

Is killed.

Is travelling on a train.

Speaks with a Scottish accent.

Is handcuffed to Hannay.

Hannay thinks she is going to kiss him.

Is married to an older man.

Has a meal in a hotel with Hannay.

Argues with Hannay.

Is kissed by Hannay when they first meet.

Is kissed by Hannay when they part.

Shoots a gun in the theatre.

Prepares a meal of herrings for Hannay.

Has a gun aimed at her in the theatre.

Says she would like some haddock.

Rebecca Dines as Pamela with Mark Anderson Phillips as Hannay ▲

TIP

Characters may be interpreted in many different ways. Some productions present the Professor as a clear villain from the first moment he is seen, while in others, he is more sympathetic and believable as an English academic, so it is a surprise when he reveals his German allegiances.

However you interpret the character, you must be able to justify your choices based on your understanding of the play.

Characterisation focus on Professor Jordan and Mrs Jordan

Professor Jordan is the villain, or antagonist, of the play. He is first mentioned by Annabella as the Englishman that she must visit at Alt-na-Shellach, but he turns out to be the 'brilliant secret agent of a certain foreign power'. He is aided by Mrs Jordan who, at first, seems to be an ordinary, gracious woman, but is revealed as the Professor's accomplice.

Both characters present a false impression at first, but then dramatically reveal their true natures. Performers must consider how their acting skills can make these revelations powerful.

Stage directions and physical skills

The stage directions give indications on how the actors can use their physical skills to create particular impressions on the audience.

Task B30

1 The chart below contains stage directions for Professor Jordan and Mrs Jordan.

Use it to note physical skills that actors could use and the impact these will have.

Stage directions	Physical skills	Impact on audience
Mrs Jordan: *smiling graciously, they march through several enormous rooms.* (page 36)	*Assumes the attitude of a good hostess, smiling and making eye contact with Hannay. She will gesture gracefully to the rooms as they walk past them. She is clearly leading him through a huge house, walking at a brisk pace.*	*Seems to be an ordinary, pleasant person and gives the illusion that Hannay is safe at last. The way she greets him will indicate that she is used to having guests and that her house is something of a showpiece — quite a contrast to the Crofter's cottage.*
Mrs Jordan: *She has second thoughts. Closes the door.* (page 36)		
Professor: *seated in an armchair.* (page 37)		
Professor: *The professor stands. Still smiling.* (page 38)		
Professor: *He holds up his own little finger. It is cut off at the knuckle.* (page 39)		
Professor: *pulls out a gun.* (page 39)		
Mrs Jordan: *She takes the gun. Doesn't flick an eyelid.* (page 39)		
Professor and Mrs Jordan: *The Professor grasps Mrs Jordan's hand. They start dancing. They stamp and shout. They become wilder and wilder.'* (page 42)		

2 Carefully read Scene 18 and decide on the precise moment at which the audience learns that Professor Jordan is a secret agent. How could the use of pace, pause, gesture and stillness be used to emphasise this moment?

Professor Jordan's background

The Professor is a character of some complexity. He has successfully manipulated those around him into believing he is an English academic and a valued member of their community. When Hannay first meets him, he thinks he is an ally, so reveals his knowledge of the Thirty-nine Steps. This causes a change in the Professor's attitude. His motivations in the rest of the scene range from threatening to kill Hannay to trying to convert him to his cause. The actor's performance needs to incorporate these factors.

Task B31

1 Below is a student-style example of how he could be performed in Scene 18, page 40. Read it through and make a note of each vocal and physical skill mentioned.

2 Then add at least two more vocal or physical skills that could have been suggested.

> I want to show how cold-blooded and intelligent the Professor is, so I will have him moving in a calm way, relaxed despite the life-and-death situation. He has just threatened Hannay with a gun, but I will have him slow the pace down and say in a pleasant, matter-of-fact way, 'Unless of course you decide to join us.' He will slowly light a cigarette and hold it gracefully in a long cigarette holder as he waits for Hannay's response. His motivation is to convince Hannay to change sides, by praising the qualities he sees in him.
>
> He will continue to make eye contact with Hannay as if appraising him and will use a sarcastic tone, for example on the word 'human', when Hannay says something sentimental. During this section, his accent will gradually change from upper-class English to German, particularly evident on words like 'love'.
>
> Towards the end of the scene, when he is speaking of the master race, he will turn excitedly away from Hannay and gesture enthusiastically, indicating the strength of his beliefs.

Task B32

Read the Professor's speech in Scene 30 on page 75 (from 'I don't think so, Hannay' to 'Sorry') and write a paragraph describing how the performer could use their acting skills in this section. Remember to consider the character's motivations and what effects the actor's vocal and physical skills could create.

✓ **TEST YOURSELF B7**

Which of Professor Jordan or Mrs Jordan…?

1 Is described as 'severe-looking' and 'grey-haired'.

2 Wears tweeds.

3 Shoots Hannay.

4 Is missing part of their little finger.

5 Speaks to the Sheriff on the phone.

6 Invites Hannay to a party.

7 Does the Sheriff think is his 'best friend in the district'.

8 Speaks to the Heavies on the phone in the hotel lobby.

9 Sits in a box at the theatre.

10 Gives a secret signal to Mr Memory.

 **CHECK IT OUT**

In the *AQA GCSE Drama* coursebook, there are more ideas about Professor Jordan on page 82.

Characterisation focus on Margaret and the Crofter

The Crofter and his wife, Margaret, are a Scottish couple Hannay meets when he is evading the police. They are an unlikely pair, as the Crofter is described as 'ancient and surly', whereas Margaret is an 'incredibly pretty Scottish girl'. They also serve different dramatic functions. The Crofter is both a source of comedy and an obstacle for Hannay, while Margaret is a love interest and helps Hannay.

Robert Donat, John Laurie and Peggy Aschcroft in Hitchcock's film ▶

Task B33

One source of comedy is that the Crofter and Margaret are so ill-matched that Hannay initially mistakes Margaret for being the Crofter's daughter rather than his wife.

Draw a sketch of how each of the characters might appear in Scene 12, page 26. On your sketch, make notes of how the characters' costumes, hair and make-up might be designed, as well as their posture, body language and facial expressions to emphasise their contrasting characters.

Their backgrounds

Both the Crofter and Margaret would have Scottish accents, but their specific dialects and regional tones might be different. Crofting is hard, physical work done in isolated, rural Scottish locations. The Crofter might come from a long line of agricultural workers who have farmed the land and kept sheep and cattle. Margaret explains that she comes from Glasgow, a major city in Scotland, and she clearly misses the excitement of the shops and entertainments there. Her loneliness and unhappiness in her marriage provide motivation for her attraction to Hannay and for her efforts to help him.

Task B34

Using your understanding of the characters' backgrounds, experiment with how you would say the following lines. Make notes on:

- Accent and dialect
- Volume
- Tone
- Pace.

> Crofter: Oh most mighty and unforgiving father. (page 29)
>
> Margaret: Ye should see Sauchiehall Street on a Saturday night with all its fine shops and the trams and the lights. (page 28)

Characterisation of Mr Memory, the Compère, Dunwoody and McQuarrie

In most productions, the 'Clowns' are actors who play many roles. One of the challenges is deciding how they will use their acting skills to quickly differentiate their many characters. At several points, they are required to form a double-act where they work closely together. The first of these is Mr Memory and the Compère in Scene 2, as they perform their Music Hall act. Another double-act, needing a different type of comic performance, is made up of Dunwoody and McQuarrie in the Assembly Hall in Scene 21. The performers must discover ways of working together, including physical comedy and comic timing, in order to get the most from their roles.

Mr Memory and the Compère

An act like Mr Memory's would have been a common feature, along with magicians, jugglers and comedians, on a variety bill at a British theatre in the 1930s. The compère would be the host, responsible for introducing and, if necessary, assisting the acts.

In the script, Mr Memory and the Compère are described as wearing similar formal costumes, and both might have Cockney accents. They both use and repeat the notable 'Thankoo'. A difference between the two is revealed, however, in their reactions to the gunshot. Mr Memory is clearly distressed and begins repeating portions of his act, while the Compère takes charge and tries to calm him down.

Task B35

1 Mr Memory's skill makes him like a human computer, able to store large amounts of information in an almost superhuman way. Look closely at his speech on pages 76–77 and experiment with how the lines could be delivered in a way that emphasises his extraordinary skill.
2 Mr Memory's death is sad and touching. With a partner, read the section leading up to this on page 77, then make notes on how Hannay and the Compère might react in order to make this moment moving for the audience.

Dunwoody and McQuarrie

Dunwoody and McQuarrie are also, to an extent, performing in public. Unlike Mr Memory and the Compère, who have a smooth, well-rehearsed act, Dunwoody and McQuarrie are local figures organising a political event. Part of the humour of this scene is their lack of polish. Both are described as 'doddery', suggesting that they move stiffly and uncertainly. McQuarrie is a particularly poor speaker and is frequently interrupted by Dunwoody's demands that he speak up.

Task B36

1 With a partner, experiment with physical skills you could use for comic effect when the two men are bringing on the furniture for the speeches. For example:
   • How quickly or slowly would they do this?
   • Would they have to stop to take breaks?
   • Might something fall over?
   • Would they be impressed with each other's efforts?
2 Look at page 47, when Dunwoody interrupts McQuarrie. Experiment with the comedy of this section. For example, consider how loudly the characters might speak and at what pace.

TIP

Some productions emphasise the comic double-act by casting actors who make an amusing visual image, like other famous comic duos such as Laurel and Hardy or Morecombe and Wise. Sometimes, one of the clowns is very tall and thin, while the other is short and stout.

Laurel and Hardy in the 1937 film Way Out West ▲

Wesley Mann and Jason O'Connell, Hudson Valley Shakespeare Festival ▲

Characterisation focus on the Salesmen and the Heavies

Two other comic double-acts that the Clowns undertake are the travelling Salesmen on the train and the two Heavies who 'arrest' Hannay. The tone of these two partnerships would be very different. The Salesmen are happy, open, talkative characters, whereas the Heavies are tough, violent and perhaps not very bright. Both provide obstacles for Hannay: the Salesmen because they might discover who he is, and the Heavies because they have been ordered to kill him.

The Salesmen

From their dialogue, it is difficult to tell the two Salesmen apart. They seem to share similar attitudes and jokes, to such an extent that they frequently repeat each others' lines.

One way of creating a comic effect with the Salesmen is through vocal choices, such as using a quick pace or establishing a rhythm that is suddenly interrupted.

Task B37

1 Work with a partner to read the dialogue between the Salesmen on page 15. Try the following:
   - Read all the lines very quickly with no pauses.
   - Read the lines quickly, but choose three places to pause.
   - Have both speak with the same pitch.
   - Have one salesman speak with a very low voice and the other with a higher voice.
   - Decide on three specific movements or gestures that the Salesmen will perform in unison.
   - Have each salesman doing different gestures or movements, for example, one sits when the other stands, one leans back when the other leans forward.
2 Discuss with your partner which choices best suited the characters and what effects you could achieve.

Task B38

Read Scene 22 (page 50) and decide how the Heavies could make a strong impression on the audience through their physical presence and actions. Make notes on:
- Body language and posture
- Proximity to and interaction with Hannay
- Reactions to Pamela.

KEY TERM

Pitch: How high or low a voice is.

The Heavies

The Heavies pretend to be police officers but are in fact working for the Jordans. Hannay is suspicious of them early on, but Pamela is only convinced that they have been lying when she overhears their telephone conversation with Mrs Jordan. The Heavies, as their nickname suggests, should seem like strong, dangerous men. At the same time, however, they are rather foolish in the way they let Hannay and Pamela escape and when they speak so openly about the plot in the hotel lobby.

Task B39

Read page 54 of the script, from when the Heavies see the empty car. How could the actors create excitement and urgency through their use of vocal and physical skills? Experiment with the following:
- How loudly or softly will you speak?
- How quickly or slowly will you speak?
- What physical actions will you take to show that you are trying to find Hannay and Pamela?
- How could you use the stage space and items on it to show you are searching?
- How can you establish the comic partnership between the two Heavies?

Characterisation of the McGarrigles and minor characters

The McGarrigles are a Scottish couple who run a hotel. They are depicted as warm-hearted and friendly people. They misunderstand the relationship between Hannay and Pamela, but do what they can to help them. When performing these characters, it is useful to think how their voices and facial expressions will show their sympathy towards Hannay and Pamela.

One way to differentiate them from other characters is to exaggerate their Scottish background. Their name and their surroundings (which is introduced by Scottish pipe music) suggest this could be an important element of their characterisation.

Laura Kirman, Stephen Joseph Theatre ▲

Task B40

Explore how the McGarrigles could be costumed and performed in order to emphasise their 'Scottishness'. Consider:

- **Hair and make-up**: A stereotype of Scottish people, sometimes exaggerated for comic effect, is that they have fair skin and red hair. Is this something that you might use in your hair and make-up designs, or do you have alternative ideas of how to differentiate these characters?
- **Costumes**: Tartan fabric and checked knits are considered Scottish. Could this be worked in to your costume design?
- **Accents**: Mrs McGarrigle has such a strong accent that Hannay finds her difficult to understand. Can you study Scottish accents and think about which aspects could be exaggerated?

Small roles and multi-rolling

There are a number of other characters who make brief appearances. In order for their roles to be understood by the audience, it is necessary to find simple, bold ways of establishing the character immediately. One way of doing this is to decide on a signature posture and gesture for each character. You might decide, for example, that one character is always bent forward and wringing their hands, while another might stand with their legs apart with a hand on one hip.

Task B41

1 Write a sentence, or draw and label a sketch, describing the posture and a possible gesture for each of these characters:
   - Milkman
   - Mrs Higgins
   - Paperboy
   - Policeman
   - Sheriff
   - Inspector.
2 Then suggest for each character:
   - One important costume item or prop
   - One distinctive aspect of their voices.

Use of posture, body language, gestures and expressions

How a performer stands, moves and gestures will convey information and messages to the audience, including the character's age, social status, mood or attitude.

Task B42

Look at the production photographs below and then write three sentences describing the characters' physicality. Consider:

- **Posture:** Upright or slumped? Straight or at an angle? Weight evenly balanced or off balance? Head up or down? Facing the audience or another character, or looking away?
- **Stance or seated position:** Legs straight or bent? Legs close together or apart? One leg in front of the other?
- **Gestures:** Arms at the sides? Pointing? Outstretched?
- **Proximity:** Close to another character or distant from them? Touching another character?
- **Facial expressions:** Eyes wide open or closed? Smiling or sad? Relaxed or tense? Frowning?

Stephen Critchlow and Timothy Speyer

Gary Mackay and Richard Ede

TheatreWorks cast

Task B43

Draw sketches or write short descriptions to show your ideas for the posture, body language, gestures and facial expressions at the following moments:

- The Milkman's reaction in Scene 5 (page 13) when he realises Hannay has given him his own money
- Hannay's response in Scene 21 (page 50) to the 'wild applause' after his speech
- Scene 28, page 65, when Pamela overhears Heavy 2 on the telephone to Mrs Jordan.

Experimenting with vocal and physical skills

As a performer, the choices you make for using vocal and physical skills will depend on what your character is feeling and thinking, as well as the effects you wish to convey to the audience.

Task B44

1 Experiment with performing the following line (from Scene 18, page 28) in a number of different ways:

> Do take a seat Mr Hannay.

Perform this as if you:
- Are frightened and want to prevent Hannay from speaking
- Are fond of Hannay and are going to tell him a story
- Want to unsettle him
- Are playing games with him
- Think Hannay is ill or tired, so shouldn't be standing
- Are annoyed and are going to argue with Hannay
- Are stalling before saying what you really think
- Are busy and thinking about something else
- Want to put Hannay at ease
- Are asserting your authority and stressing how powerless Hannay is.

2 How did your understanding of motivations affect your physical and vocal choices? Did you…?
- Speak more loudly or softly
- Talk more quickly or hesitantly
- Help the person into the chair or point to where the chair was
- Stress a certain word
- Move closer or further away as you spoke
- Make or avoid eye contact.

Task B45

1 Look closely at Scene 3, pages 9–10, between Annabella and Hannay. Consider how the performer playing Annabella could use vocal and physical skills to convey that she:
- Is highly intelligent
- Is skilful at getting people to do what she wants
- Knows she is attractive to men
- Is on an important mission
- Knows she is in danger.

2 After experimenting with the scene, write a paragraph explaining how the performer playing Annabella could use acting skills including:

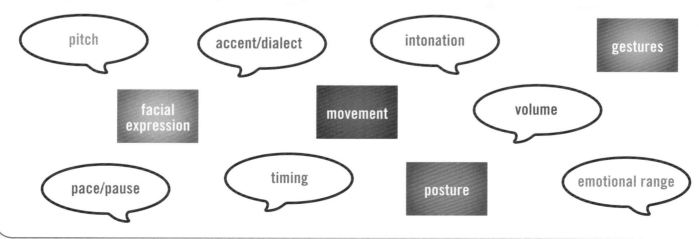

pitch

accent/dialect

intonation

gestures

facial expression

movement

volume

pace/pause

timing

posture

emotional range

Task B46

Read the description below of how a performer playing Hannay in Scene 3 might play the role. Mark each vocal skill with **V** and each physical skill with **P**. Alternatively, use different-coloured highlighters to show vocal and physical skills.

I want to convey that Hannay is curious about Annabella and attracted to her. He will tend to use humour and understatement to disguise his interest. After his more relaxed physical movement at the beginning of the scene, he will become tense when he looks out the window and turns around, dramatically making eye contact with Annabella. When he repeats the word 'involved', he will emphasise it to show that it has two meanings – involved with her mystery and involved with her romantically. He will pause before exclaiming more loudly and urgently, 'Tell me!' He will shrug and say in a light, off-hand manner, 'What's that, a pub?', showing his sense of humour. After the fast-paced dialogue, there will be a pause before he says, 'Of course.' He and Annabella will stare into each other's eyes and he will step closer to her, indicating the attraction between them.

Amelia Donkor as Pamela, Stephen Joseph Theatre ▲

KEY TERM

Phrasing: How the words in a line of speech are grouped together. For example, whether a line is said on a single breath or broken into fragments.

Task B47

Match the character and appropriate scene to the following physical skills. (There might be more than one suitable answer.) Who might...?

- Take a gun from someone   *Mrs Jordan, Scene 18*
- Run through the streets
- Hit someone
- Remove their glasses
- Blow smoke in someone's face
- Stagger in pain, fear or shock
- Touch someone seductively
- Bring in a tray of sandwiches
- Tremble in fear
- Stare at someone in disbelief
- Handle a prop
- Have a physical fight with someone.

Revealing characterisation through vocal effects on dialogue

Task B48

Now you have tried out a range of vocal acting techniques, choose some that you could use on the lines in the table on the following page to express the character and their situation.

Try to include two examples of vocal skills for each line. Think about:

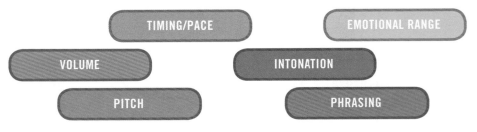

TIMING/PACE   EMOTIONAL RANGE

VOLUME   INTONATION

PITCH   PHRASING

Continued on next page ▶

Line	Vocal skills	Details and explanation of what these choices will express to the audience
(Scene 2) Compère: And now with your kind attention I have the immense honour and privilege to presentin' to you one of the most remarkable men ever in the whole world.	Volume: Increasing.	I will speak loudly and grow louder as I build up to 'whole world' to impress the audience with the act I am introducing.
	Accent: Cockney.	I will have a Cockney accent, suitable for the Cockney Music Hall setting.
	Emphasis: Stressing key words.	I will emphasise words like 'immense', 'privilege' and 'remarkable' to create excitement for the audience as if they were sitting in a 1930s music hall.
(Scene 4) Annabella: There is a man in Scotland... only a matter of days.		
(Scene 9) Pamela: This is the man you want Inspector.		
(Scene 30) Professor: You thought you found love, Hannay?		

Revealing characterisation through physical effects on dialogue

Task B49

Choose at least two physical skills you could use on the lines in the table below to express the character and their situation. Think about, for example:

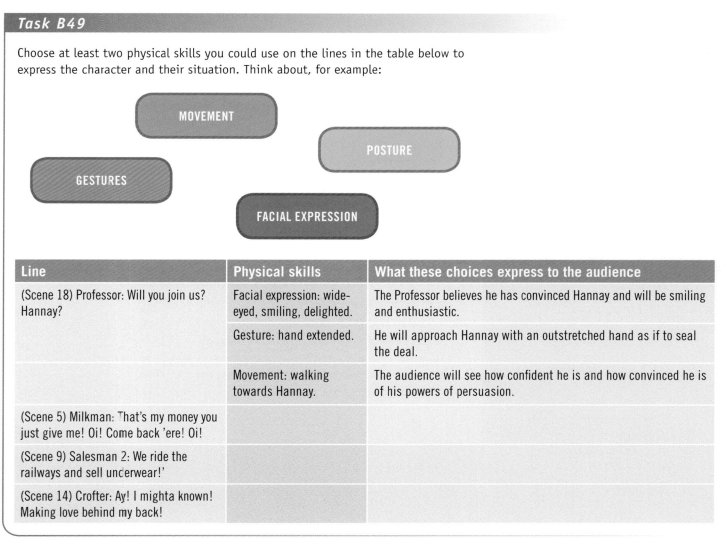

MOVEMENT

POSTURE

GESTURES

FACIAL EXPRESSION

Line	Physical skills	What these choices express to the audience
(Scene 18) Professor: Will you join us? Hannay?	Facial expression: wide-eyed, smiling, delighted.	The Professor believes he has convinced Hannay and will be smiling and enthusiastic.
	Gesture: hand extended.	He will approach Hannay with an outstretched hand as if to seal the deal.
	Movement: walking towards Hannay.	The audience will see how confident he is and how convinced he is of his powers of persuasion.
(Scene 5) Milkman: That's my money you just give me! Oi! Come back 'ere! Oi!		
(Scene 9) Salesman 2: We ride the railways and sell underwear!'		
(Scene 14) Crofter: Ay! I mighta known! Making love behind my back!		

Task B50

1 Make plans for a response to four or five of these exam-style sample questions.

2 Then choose one to answer in full. Make sure that you write about both physical and vocal skills and what impact your choices will have on how the audience understands the character.

3 Go through your answer, giving yourself a tick each time you have noted particular acting skills and effects.

TIP

Imagine yourself fully as a performer in the named role. Whenever possible, write in the first person, for example 'I would use my voice to...'

Exam-style example question: Component 1, Section B, Question 2

A Focus on Scene 1, page 2.

You are performing the role of **Hannay**.

Describe how you would use your vocal and physical skills to perform the line below, and explain the effects you want to create.

'Find something to do, you bloody fool!' [8 marks]

B Focus on Scene 13, page 28.

You are performing the role of **Margaret**.

Describe how you would use your vocal and physical skills to perform the line below, and explain the effects you want to create.

'Do London ladies look beautiful?' [8 marks]

C Focus on Scene 14, page 31.

You are performing the role of the **Crofter**.

Describe how you would use your acting skills to perform the line below, and explain the effects you want to create.

'Ay! To bring shame and disgrace upon my house!' [8 marks]

D Focus on Scene 19, page 44.

You are performing the role of the **Sheriff**.

Describe how you would use your vocal and physical skills to perform the line below, and explain the effects you want to create.

'Do you think I enjoy playing for time with a MURDERER!!!' [8 marks]

E Focus on Scene 21, page 46.

You are performing the role of **McQuarrie**.

Describe how you would use your acting skills to perform the line below, and explain what effects you want to achieve.

'Ah! He's here! He's here! Thank the Lord! Thank the Lord! Thank the Lord!' [8 marks]

F Focus on Scene 29, page 68.

You are performing the role of **Pamela**.

Describe how you would use your vocal and physical skills to perform the line below, and explain the effects you want tc create.

'I'm sorry. I feel such an awful fool for not having believed you.' [8 marks]

G Focus on Scene 30, page 75.

You are performing the role of the **Professor**.

Describe how you would use physical and vocal skills to perform the line below, and explain the effects you want to create.

'You don't destroy me, Hannay!' [8 marks]

Sample answer: Component 1, Section B, Question 2

You are performing the role of **Pamela**.

Describe how you would use your acting skills to perform the line below, and explain the effects you want to create.

'I'm cold and I'm wet and I'm miserable and my wrist hurts and I didn't do anything to hurt you!' [8 marks]

At this point in the play, Pamela is completely exasperated by the situation she finds herself in: handcuffed to a strange man and lost on the cold, wet moors. Pamela is independent-minded and not afraid of speaking up. ① She will speak in her usual upper-middle-class English accent, but more loudly and forcefully than usual. Her voice will be high-pitched and indicate the anger that she is feeling. ②

She will also be feeling sorry for herself. She will hunch her shoulders and be shivering as she emphasises the words 'cold' and 'wet'. ③ She will make eye contact on the word 'you', making clear that she blames Hannay for their situation. ④

As Pamela is handcuffed to Hannay, when she tries to move away from him at the end of the line, she will be pulled back abruptly, creating a comic effect as she ends up even closer to him than her original position. ⑤

① Shows an understanding of the play, scene and character.

② Includes vocal skills (accent, volume, pitch, emotional range).

③ Includes physical skills (posture) and vocal skills (emphasis).

④ Describes physical skill (eye contact) and its effect (relationship with Hannay).

⑤ Considers physical skills (movement) and effect (comic).

 TIP

When writing about how an actor might use physical and vocal skills, think about the effects that you might want to achieve, such as:

- An aspect of the character's background (social class, education, age, occupation)

- A character's emotional or physical state (angry, sad, happy, in love, grief-stricken, cold, warm, wet, exhausted)

- Having an effect on or reaction to another character (dominate, surrender to, woo, delay, escape, blame, amuse, convince, shame)

- An aspect of the style or genre of the play (comic, exaggerated, tense, romantic).

TIP

When writing about what you want to achieve through performance, production and staging, effects to consider could include:

- Comedy
- Tension
- Romance
- Surprise
- Fear
- Sympathy
- Pity
- Alarm
- Anticipation.

Use of performance space and interaction with other characters

You might be asked how an actor could use the performance space and interaction with other characters in relation to a specific extract from the play. You will need to show that you understand how the characters' movements, actions, reactions and interactions contribute to an audience's understanding of the play. Involved in this will be consideration of the particular effects, such as tension, surprise, comedy, romance or sympathy, that the performers might try to achieve.

In *The 39 Steps*, there are scenes that are comic, romantic or tense. There are scenes that involve many characters and complicated movements and simple scenes with just two characters. In order to convey the relationships between the characters and the action of the story, you must consider how the performance space can be used and how the characters might interact with each other.

Task B52

Focus on Scene 30, page 75. Copy another version of the staging configuration from Task B51 and consider how the use of performance space and interaction between the characters can create tension and excitement. Use arrows to indicate key moments when the characters might move. Indicate the following:

- Where will Mr Memory, the Professor, Pamela and Hannay be positioned at the beginning of this section?
- How will Mr Memory react when he sees the Professor?
- How can the Professor's movements show his reaction to being exposed?
- How do Pamela and Hannay react when the Professor points the gun at her?
- How might the fight between the Professor and Hannay be staged?

Task B51

1 Focus on Scene 9, page 21, from when Hannay escapes down the corridor to the end of the page.
Below is a thrust staging configuration. Copy the diagram and then draw and label where you would position the actors to achieve the following effects:

- Where will Hannay be positioned at the beginning of the scene?
- Where will you place the Policemen to convey that Hannay is trapped?
- Where on the stage will Pamela appear?
- How will Hannay's movements show the choice he makes to escape the Policemen?

- What interaction will there be between Pamela and Hannay?

2 Look closely at 'Policeman 1: Excuse me...' to 'Both policemen march towards him.' Make notes on what movements and actions could be used to create tension. Consider:

- What are the Policemen's postures? How might they seem particularly forceful or frightening?
- How does Hannay react when he sees the first Policeman? How do his movements, facial expression or posture change?
- What is his reaction when he sees the second Policeman?
- How might Hannay's expression, movements or gestures show how he feels when he hears his name spoken?
- Will the pace of his movements change during this section? What is the effect of the moment when he 'freezes'?
- What is the proximity of the Policeman to Hannay at the end of this section?

Characters' movements in *The 39 Steps*

Task B53

Use your knowledge of the play to consider character movements. Find at least one instance when a character displays the following movements and actions:

- Gives a character an overcoat.   *Margaret, Scene 14*
- Points a gun at someone.
- Runs away.
- Falls asleep.
- Falls to the ground.
- Embraces another character.
- Holds hands with another character.
- Hands something to another character.
- Dances with another character.
- Tiptoes out of a room.
- Sits on another character's lap.

Task B54

1 Look closely at Scene 25, pages 55–56. Imagine you are playing Pamela and make notes on the following scenarios. Use the vocabulary suggestions on the following pages to help you.

- **Proximity**: How close are you to Hannay at the beginning of this scene? Are there any moments when you move closer or attempt to move apart?
- **Levels**: Do the levels you use in this scene change, for example, when you get stuck in a bog or try to go under the stile?
- **Touch**: Hannay is described as pulling and dragging you. How do you react to this? Do you have any other physical contact with him?
- **Stage positions**: Where onstage are you at the beginning of the scene? At what points do you move to a new position?
- **Pace or style of movement**: Do you move quickly or slowly? What affects the speed of your movement? Do you pause or change tempo at any point? Is the style of your movement different from earlier in the play?
- **Reactions**: How do you respond to being handcuffed to Hannay? How do you react when you think he has a gun?

2 Continue to imagine you are playing Pamela. Again, focus on the specified extract above and answer this question:
Explain how you and the actor playing Hannay might use the performance space and interact with each other to create comedy and explore the relationship of the characters.

Jason Lott as Mrs McGarrigle, Olney Theatre Center ▸

Useful vocabulary for describing the use of stage space and interaction with other characters

When writing about how space on the stage is used, you might find that some of the words and phrases detailed here will be helpful.

Proximity

How close or far away are the characters? A character might **move closer** to another character for many reasons, including because they:

▶ Are attracted to them

▶ Want to share a secret

▶ Have few personal boundaries

▶ Want to intimidate them

▶ Are connected in some physical way.

Some reasons why a character might **move away** from another character are because they:

▶ Are frightened of them

▶ Want to keep something secret from them

▶ Need to be somewhere else.

Levels

Are characters **standing** or **sitting** on the **same level**, or is **one above the other**? The positioning of characters on different levels might involve:

▶ A **high level** to show dominance or observation

▶ A **low level** to show defeat or exhaustion, or to show respect to someone else, or to hide.

▶ Sitting down to show that a character feels comfortable or at home somewhere

▶ Standing to show respect or because their job requires it.

Touch

A significant type of **character interaction** is **touch**, which can show anything from love to hate. Some examples include:

▶ **Embracing** or **tenderly touching** to show attraction, affection or love

▶ **Pushing** or **striking** out to demonstrate dominance or anger

▶ Assisting another character by **guiding** them or **handing** them objects

▶ Being **in contact** because their jobs or an activity requires it

▶ Forced to be in contact due to some restriction of space or a physical connection.

Stage positions

In order to describe the characters' **movements**, such as entrances, exits, **crosses** and taking centre stage, it is useful to use the correct terms for stage **positions**. For example:

▶ A character might move **centre stage** or **downstage** in order to attract attention or connect with the audience.

▶ Characters might make **counter-crosses**, such as one moving **downstage right**, while another moves **upstage left**, in order to avoid each other.

▶ Characters might enter **upstage** so they face the audience as they come on or they might enter **downstage**, with their backs to the audience.

Pace and style of movement

In order to create specific effects, consider the **speed** at which movements might be done and in what **style**, for example:

▶ **Slowly**, including use of slow motion, to emphasise a moment or to create tension

▶ **Quickly**, such as fast **exaggerated** movements for comedy

▶ Slow, **graceful**, **fluid** movements to create a dreamy or romantic effect

▶ Quick, **violent** movements to demonstrate anger or force

▶ **Synchronised** movements when characters behave as a group.

Reactions

Movements or **actions** triggered by something that happens include:

▶ Something another character says or does

▶ A sound, like a scream, a whistle or an alarm

▶ The entrances or exits of other characters.

 TIP

Precise details are vital for achieving top marks. Avoid vague, general comments.

TIP

As *The 39 Steps* has many comic or exaggerated sections, experiment with how you could use the stage space or interaction between characters to heighten this effect.

Exam-style example questions: Component 1, Section B, Question 3

A You are performing the role of **Annabella**.

Focusing on Scene 2, page 5, from 'Annabella: Sheisse!' to 'They exit', explain how you and the actor playing Hannay might use the performance space and interact with each other to create excitement and surprise for your audience. [12 marks]

B You are performing the role of **Margaret**.

Focusing on Scene 14, from its opening to 'Crofter: Ach', explain how you and the actors playing Hannay and the Crofter might use the performance space and interact with each other to create tension for your audience. [12 marks]

C You are performing the role of **Hannay**.

Focusing on Scene 27, page 62, from 'Pamela scowls' to 'She tries again. Gives up', explain how you and the actor playing Pamela might use the performance space and interact with each other to create comedy for your audience. [12 marks]

D You are performing the role of the **Professor**.

Focusing on Scene 18, from 'Hannay: One little question' to the end of the scene, explain how you and the actors playing Hannay and Mrs Jordan might use the performance space and interact with each other to create tension and excitement for the audience. [12 marks]

E You are performing the role of **Pamela**.

Focusing on Scene 26, page 59, from 'She beams cheekily' to 'Pamela finishes', explain how you and the other actors in the extract could use the performance space and interact with each other to create comedy for the audience. [12 marks]

Task B55

Write a plan for each of these questions. Remember to include:

- The location of the scene (the hotel, the theatre and so on) and how that might affect positioning and movements
- What effects you want to achieve (tension, comedy, romance, sympathy, insight into the characters, conflict and so on)
- Where the scene might be positioned. (Using the whole stage? Downstage? On an upper platform?)

 TIP

The best answers are well developed and note precise details, including any changes in emotions, mood or relationships.

Sample answer: Component 1, Section B, Question 3

Focus on Scene 27, page 61.

You are playing **Hannay**.

Explain how you and the actors playing Pamela and Mrs McGarrigle might use the performance space and interact with each other to create comedy for the audience. [12 marks]

The comedy of this scene is based on the misunderstanding of Mrs McGarrigle, who thinks that Pamela and Hannay are in love. She doesn't know that they are reluctantly handcuffed together, which they must hide from her. Pamela also believes that Hannay has a gun, so she must do what I (as Hannay) say. ①

The scene is set in a hotel room and we will be standing upstage centre as if warming our hands at the fireplace, turning to smile sweetly at Mrs McGarrigle as she exits stage left. ② The second she leaves the room, our expressions will change and we will turn to face each other. This sudden change will be comic – from loving to anger. ③

When Mrs McGarrigle knocks, I will use my foot to pull a chair towards us, sit down on it and force Pamela onto my lap. She will try to get off, but I will pull her down and we will both smile cheesily again as Mrs McGarrigle enters stage left. ④ We will look slightly ridiculous with Pamela awkwardly on my lap and us both trying to hide the handcuffs. ⑤ In order to get Pamela to continue to do what I want, I will obviously nudge her with what she thinks is a gun, but is actually my pipe, so she will jump a little in surprise, while I continue to smile and look at Mrs McGarrigle. ⑥

When Pamela says, 'I say, please don't go!' there will be a long pause and I will become very still as I try to work out what to do next. Mrs McGarrigle will look at us with concern and take a step closer. ⑦

① Explains context of scene, demonstrating understanding of play.

② Describes location and stage positioning, using correct terminology.

③ Explains use of movement and comic effect.

④ Gives an example of change of levels and interaction.

⑤ Explains desired effect.

⑥ Notes subtle effects achieved through small movements.

⑦ Explains when interaction changes and leads to moments of stillness and movement.

Task B56

Focus on an extract a little later in Scene 27, page 63. As a performer playing Pamela, plan how you and the actor playing Hannay might use the performance space and interact with each other to create comedy and explore the relationship of the characters.

Consider how:

- The characters interact when Pamela takes off her stockings
- Their use of stage space and interaction change when Hannay suggests going to bed
- The actors' positioning could add to the comedy of their situation.

Interpretations of characters

The performers and creative team interpret a play, making choices about what features to emphasise in the play and its characters in order to express their understanding of and ideas about the play's meanings, moods and styles.

Task B57

Read the following interpretations of characters, that have been written from the characters' perspectives. Identify which character's feelings, thoughts and motivations are being expressed each time. In addition, try to recall scenes or lines of dialogue that might have led to these interpretations.

I am a friendly, foolish, middle-aged Scottish woman who runs an out-of-the-way hotel with my husband. I love everything that is romantic, so enjoy encouraging and protecting young lovers at our hotel. I have a strong Highlands accent and a ready smile.

My colleague and I work for the Jordans. We do any messy, dangerous work that they give us and don't ask too many questions. Some might say we aren't the brightest fellows in the world, but we get things done. I speak with a Cockney accent. I am able to disguise my criminal roots and act like a detective when I need to. As tough as I might seem, I'm also rather silly and clumsy.

I am an independent-minded woman, confident to travel alone. I was shocked when a rather good-looking man suddenly kissed me, but I am law-abiding, so promptly reported him to the police. Imagine my surprise when I ended up handcuffed to him. He could be very irritating, but there is something about him that I find attractive.

I have a most amazing skill, which I use in a music hall act. I am able to retrieve and recite volumes of information. I'm not a natural performer, so am rather stiff at times, but I have learned certain jokes and work as a team with the Compère. I am also rather naïve and don't understand the importance of the information about the engine which I am made to memorise.

I am a highly intelligent and educated agent trying to obtain the plans for a new engine which I believe will give us an advantage over our enemies. I am able to convince others that I am a friendly English professor, but, when I get agitated, my natural accent comes out. I have an imposing presence and can convince others to do what I want.

I have worked on my small plot of land all my life. My only recreation is reading the newspaper or the Bible. I pray loudly and forcefully. I managed to get myself a young wife, who does the cooking and cleaning, which makes life easier. I can always use some extra money, so am keen to get some from that young scoundrel who came by our cottage, but I don't trust him.

I speak with a German accent. I dress elegantly, befitting a glamorous agent willing to take risks to thwart those who are attempting evil. My gait is smooth and graceful. Although usually calm, I am nervous as I know I am being followed.

KEY TERM

Gait: A way of walking.

Task B58

Choose one of the following characters and write a short interpretation of them, including what motivates them and how they might move and speak:

- Hannay
- Margaret
- Mrs Jordan.

Exploring acting skills based on an extract from the play

For your final question in Section B of Component 1, you will have a choice to write about either a performance or design skill. If you choose to write about performance, you will need to discuss the acting skills necessary for a performer playing the character named in the question for both the given extract and the rest of the play.

Showing understanding of the play, the character and performance skills

Before you can consider exactly what acting skills are necessary for performing a particular character, you need to ensure that you understand the character, including:

▶ Their importance in the play

▶ Their relationships with other characters

▶ The context/s in which they are seen.

You will also need to develop your own interpretation of the character, based on your understanding of the play. This means that there is no one 'right' answer for this question. Make sure, however, that you do not contradict the facts of the play. You should be confident, for example, of how the actors will use their skills to show their age, status, emotional state and motivations as appropriate for the play.

You can build on your understanding of physical and vocal skills, including use of performance space and interaction with others. This question, however, also requires a wider understanding of the play and how the characters might change and develop during the course of the play.

Carly Lopez and Kevin Shewey of the Actors Co-op Theatre Company, with costume design by Vicki Conrad and set design by Stephen Gifford ▾

Task B59

Use this grid to make notes on key characters at three points in the play.

Character	Scene: first key moment	Second key moment	Third key moment
Hannay	1: Speaking to the audience	14: With Margaret	Scene 30
Interpretation	A restless, upper-middle-class English bachelor who yearns for adventure.	Combines Hannay's romantic and adventurous characteristics.	Hannay fulfils his role as an action hero under difficult circumstances.
Physical skills	• Movement: Begins the scene seated, but suddenly stands… • Gestures: Waves palm outstretched… • Prop use: Grabs a tumbler of Scotch and finishes it in one gulp.	• Proximity: He and Margaret stand close to each other and make eye contact. • Touch: Margaret helps him change into her husband's coat… • Pace: Moves quickly, looking for the best means of escape.	• Movement: Runs on stage… • Gesture: Points at Mr Memory, commanding him to speak. • Expressions: Excited and wild-eyed at first… • Posture: Assumes a dramatic action pose on 'Oh no you don't Professor.'
Vocal skills	• Accent: Clipped 1930s English. • Pause: After each rhetorical question.	• Volume They will both speak softly and quickly… • Tone: Playful, then tender.	• Volume: Shouting at first… • Emotional range: Desperate at first, then confident once he has been proven right by Mr Memory.
The Crofter	12: Invites Hannay to stay	13: Demands supper	14: Suspicious of Hannay, then learns the police are there
Interpretation			
Physical skills			
Vocal skills			
Annabella	2: Shoots a gun in the air at the theatre	3: Explains her dilemma to Hannay	4: With Hannay before she dies
Interpretation			
Physical skills			
Vocal skills			
Pamela	9: With Hannay and Policemen on train	25: On Moors with Hannay	27: In hotel with Hannay
Interpretation			
Physical skills			
Vocal skills			
Professor Jordan	18: Pretends to be sympathetic to Hannay	18: Reveals his real persona to Hannay	30: Shoots Mr Memory and threatens Pamela
Interpretation			
Physical skills			
Vocal skills			
Margaret	13: Interacts shyly with Hannay	13: Serves meal to Crofter and Hannay	14: Wakes Hannay and helps him to escape
Interpretation			
Physical skills			
Vocal skills			

Extending acting skills from an extract to the rest of the play

Task B60

Read Scene 25, from the beginning until 'I don't have a husband'. Experiment with different ways the roles could be performed. Then answer the following exam-style question.

> You are performing the role of **Pamela**.
> Describe how you would use your acting skills to interpret Pamela's character in this extract, and explain why your ideas are appropriate both for this extract and the play as a whole. [20 marks]

TIP

Remember to select specific lines, stage directions or moments from the play to support your ideas.

You might use a plan similar to this one.

1 Pamela's importance in the play, including her relationship with Hannay.

2 Her frustration with the situation in which she finds herself.

3 How she could use her vocal and physical skills to show her feelings towards Hannay and the difficulty of the physical conditions.

4 How she might use the stage space to show that she cannot move far from Hannay, though she might like to, and that they are outside in dark and difficult circumstances. How could she create comedy through her movements?

5 How she might use her acting skills in Scene 9, when she first meets Hannay.

6 How she could use her acting skills in Scene 29, when she discovers that Hannay was telling the truth.

7 Conclusion: How Pamela changes through the play, from identifying Hannay to the police, to being unwillingly handcuffed to him, to falling in love with and marrying him.

TIP

In the exam, you can answer either Question 4 (performance) or Question 5 (design). Whichever you choose, it will be worth the most marks in Section B, so your answer needs to be well developed, using precise details from the extract and examples of how your ideas could be used in the rest of the play.

How to create a plan for Section B, Question 4

Remember that, when planning your response for Question 4, you should make sure that you write about both the given extract and the play as a whole. Below is a suggested plan in response to the following Question 4 example:

> Focus on Scene 3, page 9.
>
> You are performing the role of **Annabella**.
>
> Describe how you would use your acting skills to interpret Annabella's character in this extract, and justify your choices both for this extract and the acting skills you would use in the rest of the play. [20 marks]

<u>Plan</u>

1 Annabella's importance in the play and the effect she has on Hannay.

2 **Extract:**

- What Annabella wants in this scene: for Hannay to assist her.
- My interpretation:

- <u>Vocal skills:</u>

– Accent: German.

– Pitch: Low, throaty.

– Emotional range: Urgent, insistent and seductive. Laughs bitterly when he suggests calling the police.

– Pause/pace: Pauses before 'involved' to suggest its double meaning. Quick-paced when she rejects calling the police. Pauses when she holds up her little finger.

- <u>Physical skills:</u>

– Posture: Drapes herself seductively on the furniture.

– Gestures: Raises hand to show little finger.

– Facial expressions: Makes eye contact and smiles at Hannay on 'involved' and 'May I stay the night?'

– Movement: Moves towards Hannay on 'May I stay the night?'.

3 **Rest of play:**

Scene 2: Introduction to her character and her surprising actions.

- **Vocal skills:**
  - Pitch/tone: Low-pitched, very polite (in contrast to shooting a gun suddenly)
  - Pace: Quick to reflect urgency of situation.
  - Volume: Stage whisper.
- **Physical skills:**
  - Posture: Strikes dramatic pose of alarm on entrance.
  - Gestures: Holds gun high in the air to shoot.
  - Touch: Takes Hannay's arm when she asks if she can come home with him.

Scene 4: Her death, both dramatic and comic.

- **Vocal skills:**
  - Volume: Softly spoken, until she shouts, 'Alt-na-Shellach!!!'
  - Tone: Breathy, sensual.
- **Physical skills:**
  - Gait: Floats in smoothly, but suddenly staggers.
  - Posture: Upright at first, then leans towards Hannay as if to kiss him.
  - Movement: Graceful before suddenly collapsing, trapping Hannay in his chair.
  - Touch: Holds his hand and then dies in his arms.

4 **Conclusion:**

Comedy is created by Annabella's exaggerated seductiveness, as well as her sudden, unexpected death.

Task B61

Use the template below to create your own plan for one of the exam-style questions that follow:

1 Character's importance in play. How they are perceived by other characters and the audience:
2 What the character wants in this extract:
3 What the character is doing to get what they want:
4 Your interpretation of the character:
5 Extract:
   - Vocal skills:
   - Physical skills:
6 Rest of play:
   - Vocal skills:
   - Physical skills:
7 Conclusion:

LOOK HERE

For more examples and advice on creating plans in the exam, go to pages 137–139.

CHECK IT OUT

There is a detailed sample plan for the character of Margaret on page 86 of *AQA GCSE Drama*.

Exam-style example questions: Component 1, Section B, Question 4

A Focus on Scene 4, pages 10–11, from the opening of the scene to 'Hannay: Golly!'

You are performing the role of **Richard Hannay**.

Describe how you would use your acting skills to interpret Hannay's character in this extract and in the rest of the play. Justify why your ideas are appropriate for this character. [20 marks]

B Focus on Scene 14, page 31, from 'Crofter: Ay! I mighta known!' to 'Crofter: Don't be funny wi' me!'

You are performing the role of the **Crofter**.

Describe how you would use your acting skills to interpret the Crofter's character, and explain why your ideas are appropriate both for this extract and the play as a whole. [20 marks]

C Focus on Scene 29, page 68, from 'Pamela: Morning' to 'Pamela: I'm sorry.'

You are performing the role of **Pamela**.

Describe how you would use your acting skills to interpret Pamela's character, and explain why your ideas are appropriate both for this extract and the rest of the play. [20 marks]

D Focus on Scene 18, page 38, from 'Professor: So sorry to have kept you' to 'Professor: Go on.'

You are performing the role of **Professor Jordan**.

Describe how you would use your acting skills to interpret the Professor's character in this extract and in the rest of the play. Justify why your ideas are appropriate for this character. [20 marks]

Task B62

1 Use your plan from Task B61 and answer one of the questions above as timed writing practice.
2 Write your own questions for these extracts, but focus on the other characters in the scenes, such as Annabella, Hannay and Margaret.
3 Use your questions for practice in planning and timed writing.

Sample answer: Component 1, Section B, Question 4

Focus on Scene 21, page 49, from 'Pamela reappears' to 'Hannay carries on, playing for time. But inspired too.'

You are performing the role of **Richard Hannay**.

Describe how you would use your acting skills to interpret Hannay's character in this extract and in the rest of the play. Justify why your ideas are appropriate for this character.

In my interpretation, Hannay should be a dashing, romantic hero, but also faintly absurd, as he is caught up in physical comedy and misunderstandings. In this scene, his motivations are to escape, but he also gets carried away expressing his patriotic ideas. ①
Throughout the play, I will speak in a slightly old-fashioned upper-class English accent, which suits words I use in this speech, such as 'chap' and 'old ticker'. ②

At the beginning of the extract, I am slightly thrown by Pamela's appearance and will pause and stutter slightly. I will lose my train of thought, so speak more hesitantly on 'well the last day really' and repeat myself on 'the odd thing' showing I don't know what to say. I begin to speak with more confidence and emotion on 'stirs the old bones'. ③

At this point, I will be leaning forward against the lectern, making eye contact with the audience, a keen wide-eyed expression on my face. ④ As I continue with the lines, which I am supposedly improvising on the spot, I will look around the room nervously wondering if someone is coming to arrest me. ⑤ However, when the music comes up under my speech, I will get carried away, and almost forget that I am in fear for my life. I will be speaking from the heart – loudly, with a warm, enthusiastic tone. I will raise both hands up on the words 'A good world!' ⑥ This confident delivery will justify the enthusiastic reception that my speech receives, but also be faintly absurd as the audience will be aware that I am making it up on the spot, basing most of my speech on events that have recently happened to me, which will add to the comedy. ⑦

My ability to react quickly to extreme situations is seen at several other points of the play, such as the train scene and the McGarrigle hotel. ⑧ In the train scene, for example, I will use movement and facial expressions to show the danger I am in by...

① Interprets Hannay with some subtlety.

② Identifies vocal skill (accent) and justifies it, giving precise details.

③ Describes vocal skills (pace/pause), justifying choices and giving precise details.

④ Notes physical skills (posture, eye contact, facial expression).

⑤ Describes and justifies movement (looking around).

⑥ Describes a change in voice (tone) and physical skill (gesture).

⑦ Explains and justifies why choices are appropriate.

⑧ Begins to apply ideas to the rest of the play.

TIP

This response opening suggests how you might write about the specified extract, but you should note that the question also asks for acting ideas about the rest of the play as well.

Exploring design skills based on an extract from the play

If you decide to answer Question 5 (design) rather than Question 4 (performance), you will need to choose one design specialism and explain how you would use it to support the action of the extract and the rest of the play.

Among the design choices you could make are:

costume   set   lighting   sound   puppetry

Whichever design specialism you choose to focus on, there are several points you should consider.

TIP

Unless otherwise specified, Question 5 will not restrict you to the given context of the play (unlike Question 1). You might choose to reflect the play's actual context, or you could create a more stylised or symbolic use of design to emphasise the play's themes or moods or to make it relevant to a particular modern audience.

KEY TERMS

Stylised: Non-realistic, heightened, exaggerated; done in a particular manner that perhaps emphasises one element.

Symbolic: Using something to represent something else. A symbolic stage design, for example, might be a non-naturalistic design to suggest something about the play and its themes.

The **technical requirements** of your design

- Your design should be an achievable creation rather than an impossible wish list.
- You need to show that you have at least a basic understanding of how your design will work on stage.
- You should use the correct technical terminology in describing your design.

Your **concept**

This is your overall approach to explain how your design will enrich the production, such as drawing out the play's themes and the location and the period in which you are setting it.

Your **inspiration**

You might also want to mention what has inspired your design, such as your understanding of the context of the play, your interpretation of the play's style, or the influence of the work of other designers or artists, to show that you understand the creative process of creating theatre.

How your design is **appropriate** for the extract and the rest of the play

You need to demonstrate that you understand not only the specific demands of the extract, but other key moments in the play that would be supported by your design.

Triad Stage production ▲

Writing about costume design

When describing your ideas for costumes, you might consider:

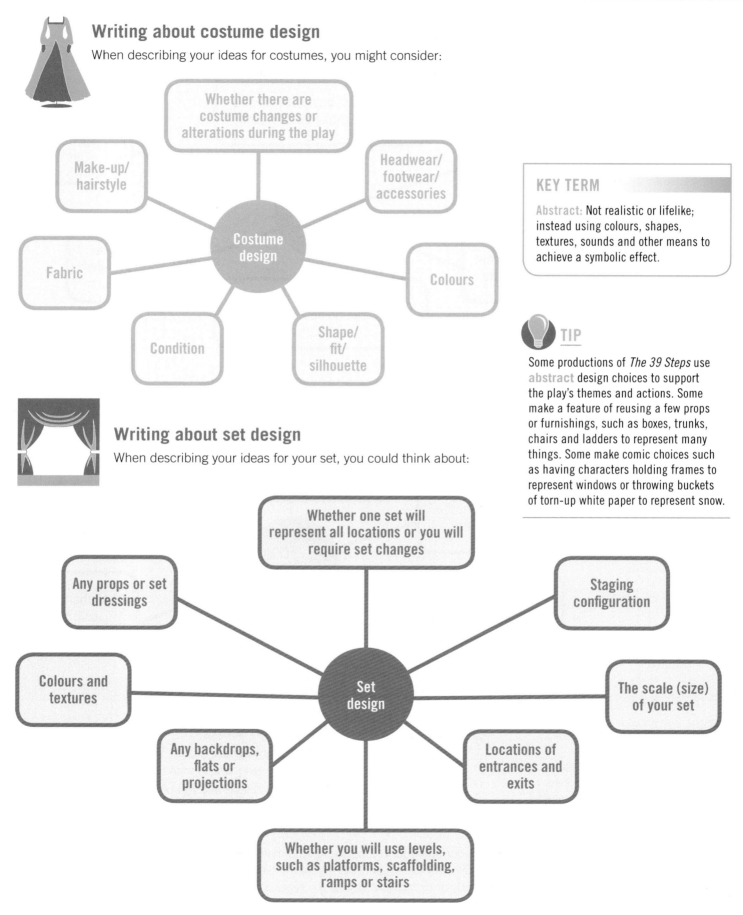

- Whether there are costume changes or alterations during the play
- Make-up/hairstyle
- Headwear/footwear/accessories
- Fabric
- Costume design
- Colours
- Condition
- Shape/fit/silhouette

Writing about set design

When describing your ideas for your set, you could think about:

- Whether one set will represent all locations or you will require set changes
- Any props or set dressings
- Staging configuration
- Colours and textures
- Set design
- The scale (size) of your set
- Any backdrops, flats or projections
- Locations of entrances and exits
- Whether you will use levels, such as platforms, scaffolding, ramps or stairs

KEY TERM

Abstract: Not realistic or lifelike; instead using colours, shapes, textures, sounds and other means to achieve a symbolic effect.

TIP

Some productions of *The 39 Steps* use abstract design choices to support the play's themes and actions. Some make a feature of reusing a few props or furnishings, such as boxes, trunks, chairs and ladders to represent many things. Some make comic choices such as having characters holding frames to represent windows or throwing buckets of torn-up white paper to represent snow.

Writing about lighting design

When describing your ideas for lighting design, you might include:

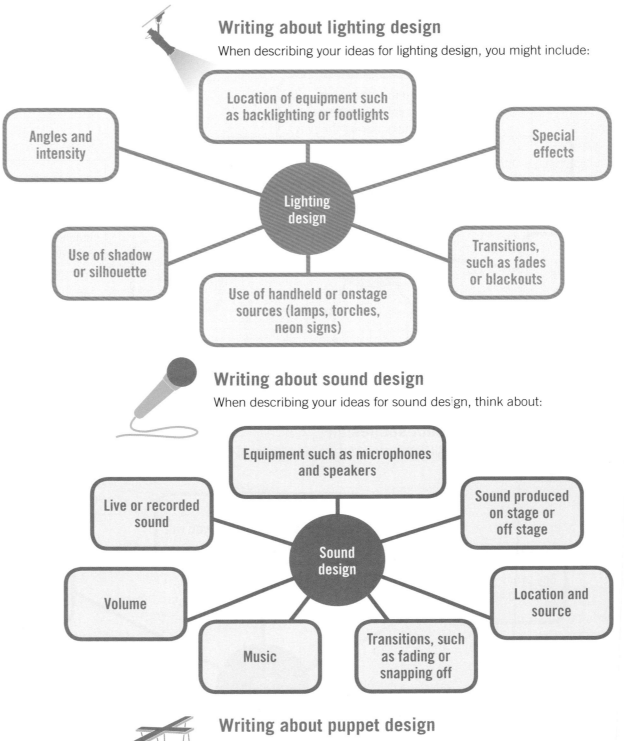

Location of equipment such as backlighting or footlights

Angles and intensity

Special effects

Lighting design

Use of shadow or silhouette

Transitions, such as fades or blackouts

Use of handheld or onstage sources (lamps, torches, neon signs)

Writing about sound design

When describing your ideas for sound design, think about:

Equipment such as microphones and speakers

Live or recorded sound

Sound produced on stage or off stage

Sound design

Volume

Location and source

Music

Transitions, such as fading or snapping off

TIP

Your design does not need to reflect previous productions of *The 39 Steps*. You might arrive at an original concept which will convey the play's meaning to an audience in a highly effective and creative way. Your design might combine naturalistic and stylised features and could use modern technology.

Writing about puppet design

If you choose to write about puppet design, you should consider the type of puppets you will create. These could include:

▸ Shadow puppets
▸ Hand puppets
▸ Marionettes.
▸ Hand and rod puppets
▸ Backpack puppets

Consider how your puppets might be made and operated and how they will add to the selected extract and the rest of the play. For example, how could they add to the comedy or excitement or help to create a setting?

Design ideas for an extract and the whole play

Task B63

Read Scene 10, pages 24–25. Then complete the following grid with design ideas for each of the specialisms.

	Design ideas and challenges of extract	Examples	Details in extract	Rest of play (pick key moments to discuss in detail)
Costume	• Costume for Hannay. • Uniforms for the Policemen.	Fabrics: Colours: Fit/condition: Footwear/accessories:		
Set	• Forth Bridge. • Outdoor night-time setting.	Staging configuration: Colours: Materials: Levels: Props:		
Lighting	• Night-time, foggy. • Blackout.	Colours: Angles/intensity: Special effects: Transitions:		
Sound	• Wind. • Creaking girders. • Hannay's descent and splash. • Morse Code. • Radio announcer's voice.	Volume: Live or recorded: On stage or off: Transitions:		
Puppetry	Large model of Forth Bridge to contrast with small marionette of Hannay.	Materials: Size: Fabrics: How it will be operated:		

Naturalistic or stylised designs?

Task B64

Some productions of *The 39 Steps* use authentic, naturalistic costumes, while others choose to create comically exaggerated outfits. Read the sample ideas below and decide which, if any, of these agree with your own ideas for the play. Then sketch your ideas for a costume for Hannay or Annabella in line with your concept for the play.

> To emphasise romance, I will have Annabella and Pamela dressed in highly flattering and beautiful clothing and Hannay will look very smart and dashing.

> All of the costumes are in black, white and grey, so the show looks like an old black-and-white film.

> The costumes have an exaggerated silhouette with padded shoulders and long, lean lines.

> The costumes are typical 1930s fashions, but have unusually bright colours and prints to highlight the comic nature of the piece.

> To draw attention to the multi-rolling, I will have everyone except Hannay with one basic outfit, over which they will simply add key accessories or costume items, such as hats, aprons or coats.

> I will have Hannay dressed in lighter tweeds than the other male characters to make him stand out. The Professor and other 'bad' characters will be dressed in dark colours.

Task B66

1 Use the staging configuration of a theatre in the round to sketch a set design for the following four moments in the play:

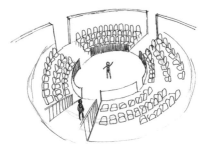

- Annabella's death in Hannay's flat in Scene 4 (page 11)
- The Professor's study in Scene 18 (page 37)
- The Heavies' car, Scene 23 (page 52)
- The London Palladium, Scene 30 (page 71).

2 Make notes on how the set would work, for example where key furniture and props might be and where characters would be positioned for key moments.

Task B65

1 One choice you will make as a designer is how realistic or stylised you want your effects to be. Look at the following moments from the play and decide whether you want natural and believable or theatrical and stylised sound, lighting, settings or costumes at each point, and why.
   - Scene 9: The train
   - Scene 18: The Professor's study
   - Scene 33: Hannay's flat.

2 Then choose one of the scenes and write a paragraph explaining how you would apply one of the design specialisms to it, making clear how realistic or stylised it would be and how this could be accomplished in a practical way.

How to create a plan for Section B, Question 5

The following suggestion is a sample plan for answering Question 5 in the exam, with notes on what you need to consider and include.

TIP

You might choose to draw a quick sketch as part of your answer if that helps you to explain your ideas more clearly and efficiently.

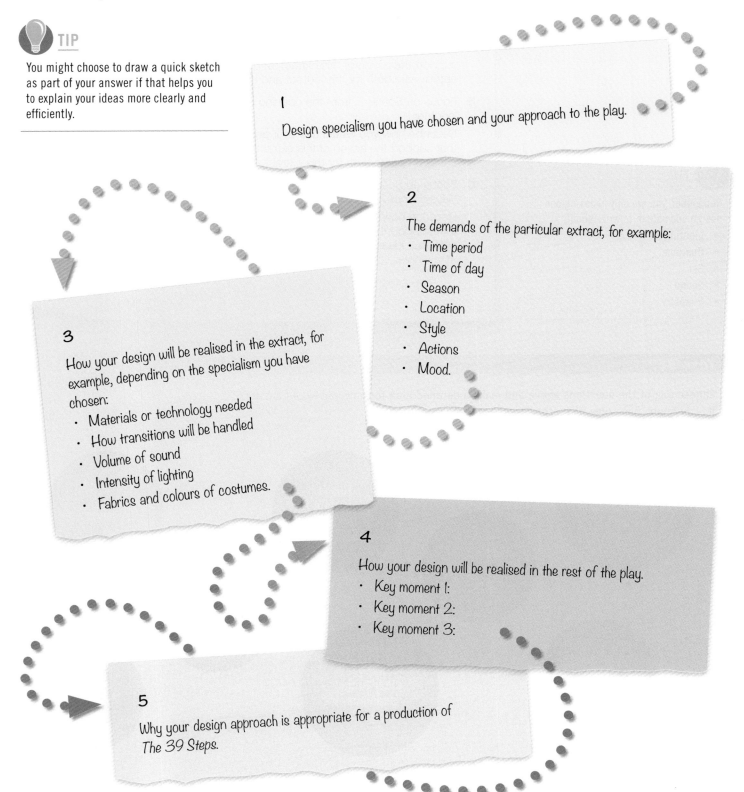

1 Design specialism you have chosen and your approach to the play.

2 The demands of the particular extract, for example:
- Time period
- Time of day
- Season
- Location
- Style
- Actions
- Mood.

3 How your design will be realised in the extract, for example, depending on the specialism you have chosen:
- Materials or technology needed
- How transitions will be handled
- Volume of sound
- Intensity of lighting
- Fabrics and colours of costumes.

4 How your design will be realised in the rest of the play.
- Key moment 1:
- Key moment 2:
- Key moment 3:

5 Why your design approach is appropriate for a production of The 39 Steps.

Exam-style example questions: Component 1, Section B, Question 5

A Focus on Scene 3, pages 6–7, from the opening to '*Telephone rings*.'

You are a designer working on one aspect of design for this extract.

Describe how you would use your design skills to create effects that support the action of this extract, and explain why your ideas are appropriate both for this extract and the play as a whole. [20 marks]

B Focus on Scene 7, from the opening to 'The Salesmen explode with laughter.'

Describe how you would use your design skills to create effects that support the action of this extract, and explain why your ideas are appropriate both for this extract and the play as a whole. [20 marks]

C Focus on Scene 17, pages 36–37, from 'Hannay: Lovely house' to '*Music stops*.'

Describe how you would use your design skills to create effects that support the mood and actions of this extract, and explain why your ideas are appropriate both for this extract and the play as a whole. [20 marks]

 TIP

Remember, you are only choosing one design specialism to write about:

- Lighting
- Costume
- Set
- Sound
- Puppetry.

Task B67

Choose one of the questions above and make a detailed plan for how you would answer it. You might find some of these sentence starters useful:

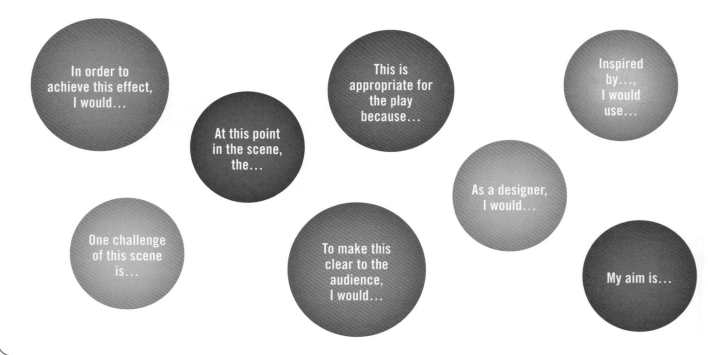

In order to achieve this effect, I would…

At this point in the scene, the…

This is appropriate for the play because…

Inspired by…, I would use…

As a designer, I would…

One challenge of this scene is…

To make this clear to the audience, I would…

My aim is…

Sample answers for Component 1, Section B, Question 5

Focus on Scene 18, pages 41–42, from 'The Professor staggers back clutching his heart' to the end of the scene.

Describe how you would use your design skills to create effects that support the mood and actions of this extract, and explain why your ideas are appropriate both for this extract and the play as a whole. **[20 marks]**

TIP

Think, 'CUT':
- **Creative**
- **Understanding**
- **Terminology.**

TIP

Remember that, in your complete answer, you will need to explain how your ideas work not just for the extract, but at other points in the play too.

Task B68

The following extracts are from student-style responses to the question above.

Read them and put:
- **C** next to creative ideas
- **U** next to any points which show understanding
- **T** next to any examples of correct terminology.

1. At this point, the act is approaching its climax and, as a lighting designer, I will want to increase the excitement and tension. In the Professor's study I will have two practical lamps – a floor lamp and a desk lamp – both with green shades. The floor lamp can be directed onto Hannay's face as if he is facing an interrogation. I will have the corners of the study underlit, to create a sense of mystery.

   When Hannay is shot, a single strobe flash will emphasise the power of the gunshot. When the door flies open, a bright column of light from fresnel lanterns in the wings will spill onto the stage. I will use a gobo to create a swirling effect, as if the wild party is just offstage. This will create excitement and a sense of danger.

   As the Jordans dance, I will backlight them with a bright red filter to exaggerate their silhouettes.

2. Sound design has an important role to play in creating the intensity and sense of danger in this scene. My concept of the play is more stylised than realistic and I want to heighten the lack of reality through music and exaggerated sound effects.

   For the gunshot, I will use an unnaturally loud recorded sound with reverb, so that Hannay's reaction can almost be in slow motion. As Hannay lays on the ground, a recording of a patriotic German song will begin to play softly, as if to show that the German agent has won. When Mrs Jordan enters, however, this will be drowned out by a burst of recorded jitterbug, such as Benny Goodman's 'Sing, Sing, Sing'. It begins with a drum solo, which could create a sense of mystery as Mrs Jordan enters, but then has a full swing orchestra that suits the Jordans' dancing. I would increase the volume of the music until the end of the scene, when it will snap off.

   My aim is to create an exciting, eerie and absurd ending to the first act.

TEST YOURSELF B8

Match the correct definition with each technical term used in theatre performance and design.

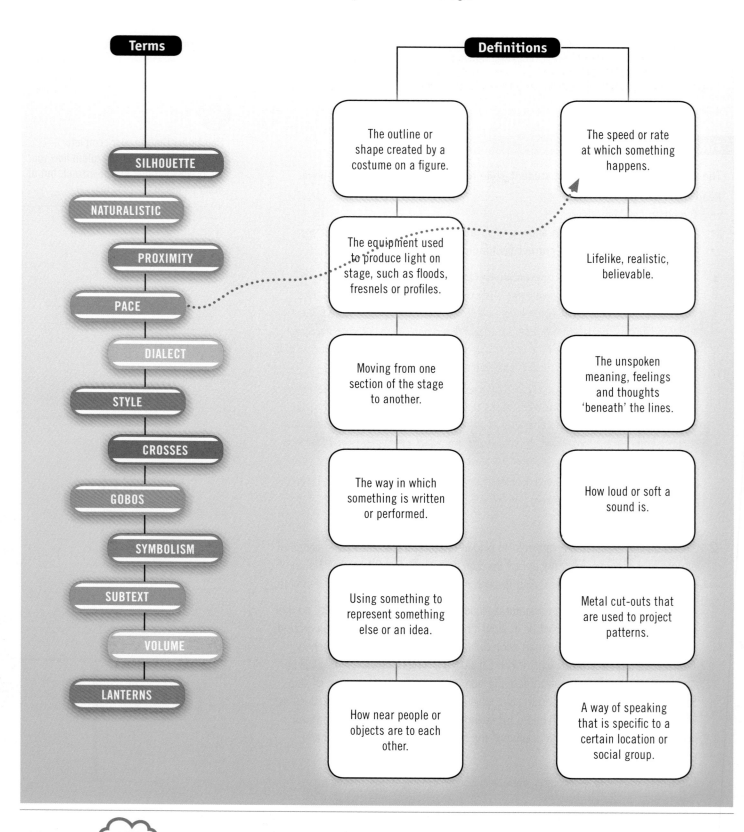

Terms

- SILHOUETTE
- NATURALISTIC
- PROXIMITY
- PACE
- DIALECT
- STYLE
- CROSSES
- GOBOS
- SYMBOLISM
- SUBTEXT
- VOLUME
- LANTERNS

Definitions

The outline or shape created by a costume on a figure.

The speed or rate at which something happens.

The equipment used to produce light on stage, such as floods, fresnels or profiles.

Lifelike, realistic, believable.

Moving from one section of the stage to another.

The unspoken meaning, feelings and thoughts 'beneath' the lines.

The way in which something is written or performed.

How loud or soft a sound is.

Using something to represent something else or an idea.

Metal cut-outs that are used to project patterns.

How near people or objects are to each other.

A way of speaking that is specific to a certain location or social group.

www.illuminatepublishing.com/drama

LEARNING CHECKLIST: SECTION B

Tick each aspect of your understanding of *The 39 Steps* if you are confident of your knowledge.

If you are unsure of anything, go back and revise.

Do you know...?

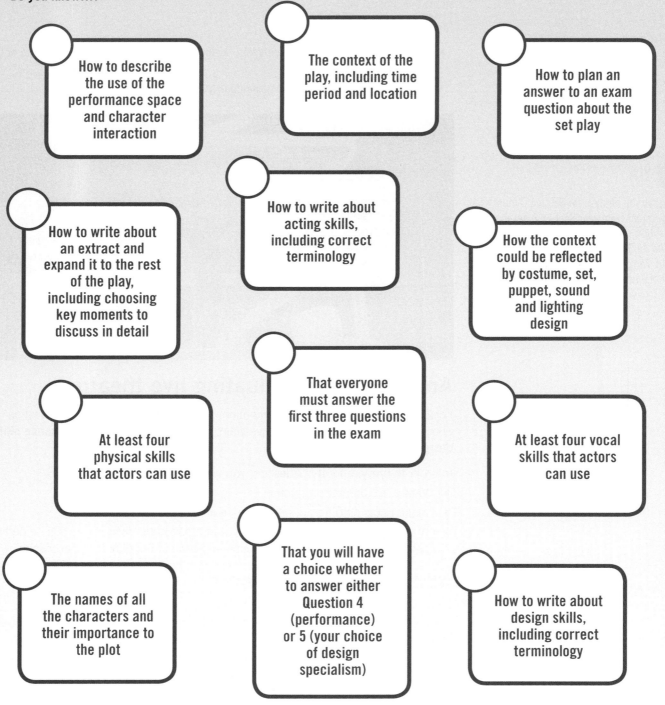

How to describe the use of the performance space and character interaction

The context of the play, including time period and location

How to plan an answer to an exam question about the set play

How to write about an extract and expand it to the rest of the play, including choosing key moments to discuss in detail

How to write about acting skills, including correct terminology

How the context could be reflected by costume, set, puppet, sound and lighting design

At least four physical skills that actors can use

That everyone must answer the first three questions in the exam

At least four vocal skills that actors can use

The names of all the characters and their importance to the plot

That you will have a choice whether to answer either Question 4 (performance) or 5 (your choice of design specialism)

How to write about design skills, including correct terminology

SECTION C

LIVE THEATRE PRODUCTION

Assessment focus:

AO3: Demonstrate knowledge and understanding of how drama and theatre is developed and performed.

AO4: Analyse and evaluate the work of others.

What the specification says...

In Section C, students answer one question (from a choice) on the work of theatre makers in a single live production.

They should be able to discuss:

- ▶ a variety of aspects of one production, giving a personal analysis and evaluation of the theatrical elements
- ▶ how successfully meaning was communicated to the audience.

TIP

The play you analyse for Section C must be different from your Section B set play. You might have seen a live production of *The 39 Steps*, but, if you are writing about *The 39 Steps* for Section B, you cannot write about it for Section C.

Noma Dumezweni in *Linda* ▶

Analysing and evaluating live theatre

For Section C of your written examination, you will need to choose one question about a theatre production you have seen. You may write about **performance skills** *or* **design skills**.

In order to prepare for this question, you will:

- ▶ View a live theatre production
- ▶ Make notes on different performance and design elements
- ▶ Analyse how the performers' acting and a particular designer's skills helped to communicate the characters, action and style of the play to the audience.

What are production elements?

When you see a performance of a play, you might notice its overall impact and whether or not you enjoyed it, rather than thinking about separating it into its many different elements. However, one of the requirements of a live theatre evaluation is to recognise how the different production elements contribute to the overall interpretation and success of the play. You must be able to consider how the performers and designers each helped to establish the meaning of the play.

There is a range of production elements to be explored when discussing live theatre.

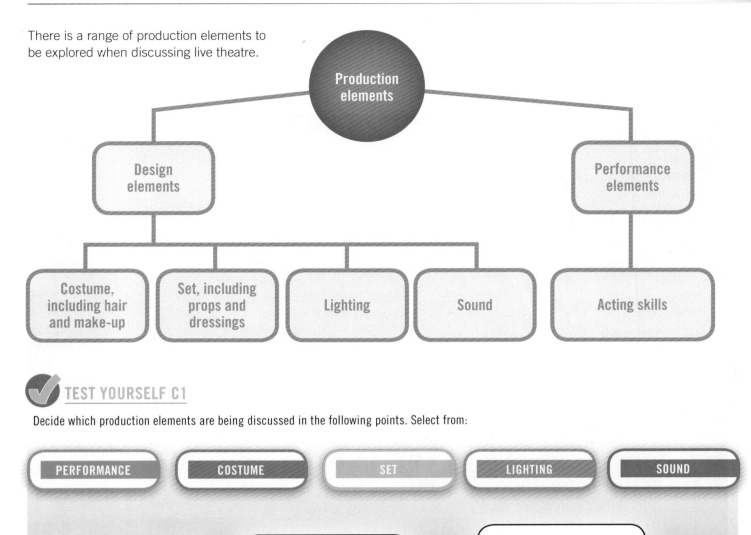

TEST YOURSELF C1

Decide which production elements are being discussed in the following points. Select from:

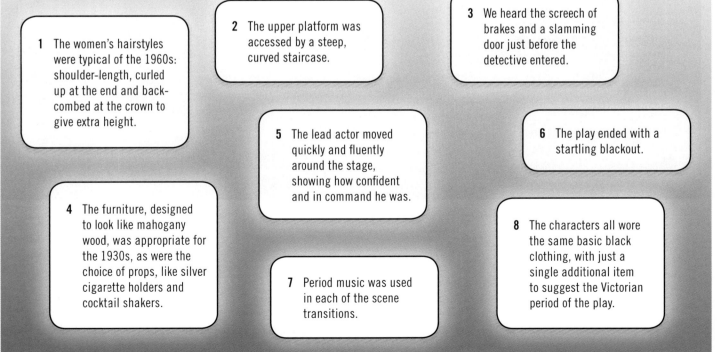

PERFORMANCE   COSTUME   SET   LIGHTING   SOUND

1 The women's hairstyles were typical of the 1960s: shoulder-length, curled up at the end and back-combed at the crown to give extra height.

2 The upper platform was accessed by a steep, curved staircase.

3 We heard the screech of brakes and a slamming door just before the detective entered.

4 The furniture, designed to look like mahogany wood, was appropriate for the 1930s, as were the choice of props, like silver cigarette holders and cocktail shakers.

5 The lead actor moved quickly and fluently around the stage, showing how confident and in command he was.

6 The play ended with a startling blackout.

7 Period music was used in each of the scene transitions.

8 The characters all wore the same basic black clothing, with just a single additional item to suggest the Victorian period of the play.

Task C1

Look at this photograph of an outdoor production of *Robin Hood*.

Make notes on the following:

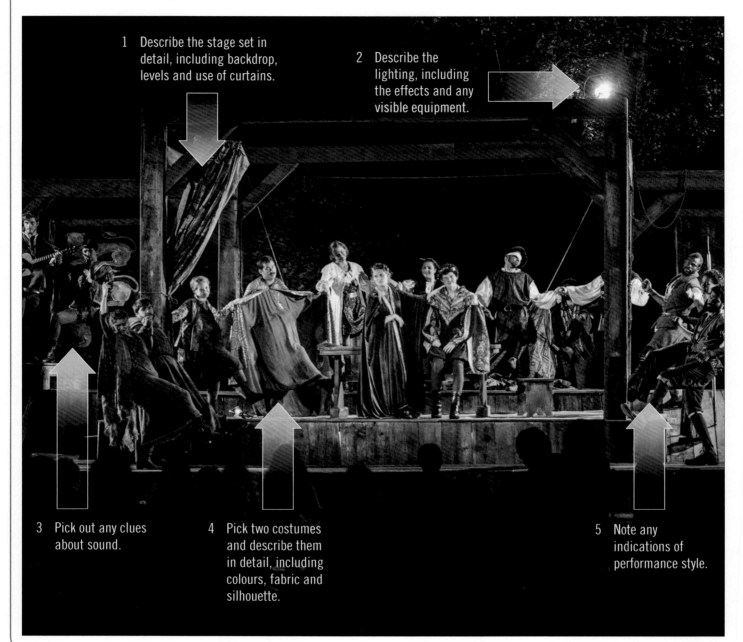

1 Describe the stage set in detail, including backdrop, levels and use of curtains.

2 Describe the lighting, including the effects and any visible equipment.

3 Pick out any clues about sound.

4 Pick two costumes and describe them in detail, including colours, fabric and silhouette.

5 Note any indications of performance style.

 TIP

In the exam, you will choose to write about either performance skills or one design skill (from a limited selection). Whichever you choose, you must provide detailed examples and use the correct terminology.

 CHECK IT OUT

There is a Live Theatre Performance Design Evaluation Sheet on page 176 of *AQA GCSE Drama*, or visit illuminatepublishing.com to download a free copy.

How to write about performance

If you choose to write about the performances you have seen in a show, you should be able to understand the range of skills used by the actors; what they were trying to achieve and how successful they were. You will need to select and include details from the performance to help to explain your ideas and, in doing so, you will need to use correct drama terminology.

Task C2

Study the photographs below and make notes on the following elements of performance, particularly in terms of how they contribute to conveying meaning:

- Facial expression
- Posture
- Stage position
- Use of gesture
- Proximity to other performers.

Also consider what the effect of the performance might be. Does it appear to be comic? Dramatic? Tense?

An open-air production of Dracula

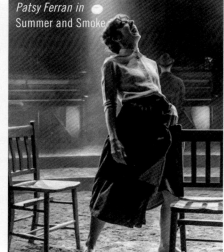

Patsy Ferran in Summer and Smoke

The National Theatre's Nine Night

What the specification says...

Students must develop knowledge and understanding of the following:

▶ How meaning is interpreted and communicated:

- Use of performance conventions
- Use of performance space and spatial relationships on stage
- Relationships between performers and audience
- Performers' vocal interpretation of character, such as accent, volume, pitch, timing, pace, intonation, phrasing, emotional range, delivery of lines
- Performers' physical interpretation of character, such as build, age, height, facial features, movement, posture, gesture, facial expression.

TIP

Throughout your exam responses, you must write as an informed drama student and audience member, not just an enthusiastic fan.

Expressing your ideas

When writing about performance skills, it is important that you describe, analyse and evaluate what you have seen, making reference to specific examples from the production.

Although the demands on professional reviewers are different in many ways from those of a drama student, they too have the task of trying to convey the quality of a performance through description and evaluation. Here are excerpts from two reviews of a performance by Patsy Ferran as Alma in *Summer and Smoke* at the Almeida Theatre in 2018:

Reviews of a performance

① Evaluative comment: 'joys'.
② Description of gestures.
③ Analysis of the effect of physical skills.

> One of the joys ① of Ferran's performance is the way her incredibly exact gestures of anxiety – her hand fluttering to her neck, the mystery of what do with one's elbows ② – also so perfectly reveal vast stores of repressed bodily longing.③ She's like a glass, brimming with water; you hold your breath for the moment it'll spill. The moment, of course, comes too late.

Holly Williams, Independent

① Evaluative introduction to overall performance: 'superb'.
② Evaluative comment on vocal skills: 'accent spot-on'.
③ Analysis of impact and precise example.
④ Evaluation: 'beautifully set down'.
⑤ Descriptive comment on vocal skills: 'nervous laugh'.
⑥ Descriptive and notes impact of gestures.
⑦ Analysis of impact of physical skills.
⑧ Descriptive comment on vocal skills: 'cackles', 'top of her voice'.
⑨ Descriptive comment on physical skills.
⑩ Analysis and evaluation of interaction: 'chemistry… off the scale'.

> Ferran is superb, ① her accent spot-on ② – even in its posh elongation of its As which stand her apart from the rest of the town ③ – and her nervousness is beautifully set down. ④ She gulps down air in shallow breaths, has a nervous laugh, ⑤ fiddles with her ring, collar and neck as she tries to talk to the one who is making her heart flutter almost visibly. ⑥ Everything about her performance is subtle but clear… Tension is wound and wound inside her and it bursts out in several separate moments of physical explosion. ⑦ At peak unhappiness she cackles at the top of her voice, ⑧ hyperventilates and stumbles around the stage. ⑨ It's like she's a firecracker, waiting to go off, and the chemistry between her and Matthew Needham's John is off the scale. ⑩

Daisy Bowie-Sell, WhatsOnStage

Task C3

Read the following extract from a candidate-style response about the same performance. Use the suggestions for improvement when evaluating your own writing, and then make the necessary changes.

> I really liked the actor's performance as Alma. She looked like I thought the character would look and she was both funny and sad. ① She was wearing the same white blouse and dark skirt throughout, which was a bit funny as I thought she should change outfits more because the action took place over several weeks. ② She seemed to like the actor playing the doctor a lot ③ and their scenes together were very interesting. ④ She created an effect ⑤ when she spoke loudly. Sometimes her gestures seemed a bit extreme to me, ⑥ but overall I really liked her work and would like to see her doing more plays. ⑦

① Too general – give examples.
② This is suitable if you chose to write about costume design, but not appropriate for a performance answer.
③ Don't confuse the actor with the character!
④ Why were they interesting? Examples needed.
⑤ What effect was created? Tension? Fear? Humour? Sympathy? Pity?
⑥ What were the gestures and why, in your opinion, didn't they work?
⑦ Concentrate on the performance you saw, rather than general observations.

CHECK IT OUT

See pages 167–174 of *AQA GCSE Drama* for more guidance on writing about performance for Section C.

Aspects of characterisation in performance

Task C4

1 Choose a key character from the play you have seen and write a three-sentence introduction to the character. Include:
   - Why the character is important in the play. (Are they the protagonist? Do they provide comic relief? Are they the antagonist or villain? Are they a character to whom the audience can relate?)
   - The character's status, background and relationships with other characters.
   - What the character's motivations are. (What do they want?)

2 Choose three of the sentence starters on the following page and use them in a second paragraph about how the actor portrays the character.

Meera Syal in Behind the Beautiful Forevers ▲

To examine and discuss a character portrayal, you need to consider how the performer has created the character. In order to do this, you should indicate that you are able to:

▸ Understand the character
▸ Describe and analyse how the performer used their skills to portray the character
▸ Evaluate how successful they were in the portrayal.

Some aspects of characterisation you might consider are the character's:

▸ Status or social background
▸ Relationship with other characters
▸ Personality and/or attitudes
▸ Appearance, including age, gender, height and build
▸ Relationship to their stage environment, including use of stage space and props.

Useful vocabulary for discussing characterisation

You might be asked how an actor has interpreted a role. This means how they have put across their understanding of the playwright's, director's and their own ideas for the character. What aspects of the character has the actor chosen to highlight and what performance techniques are they using to accomplish this? If the actor is interpreting a villainous, comic or romantic character, for example, how have they used their acting skills to do this?

When writing about how a character has been brought to life, you might find that the words offered here will be helpful.

> **SUBTEXT**
> The unspoken meaning, feelings and thoughts 'beneath' the lines

> **MOTIVATION**
> What a character wants or needs in a scene

> **STYLE**
> The manner in which something is performed, such as naturalistically or comically

Sentence starters such as these can help you to structure your writing.

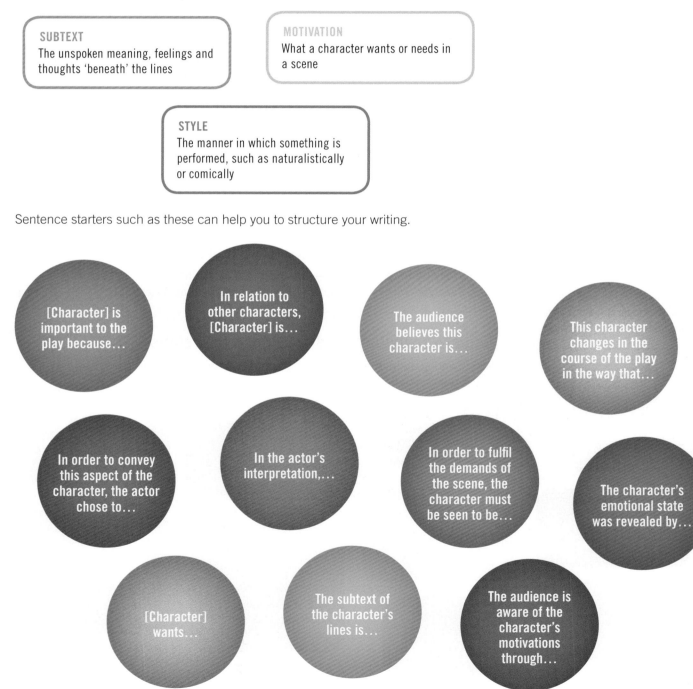

[Character] is important to the play because…

In relation to other characters, [Character] is…

The audience believes this character is…

This character changes in the course of the play in the way that…

In order to convey this aspect of the character, the actor chose to…

In the actor's interpretation,…

In order to fulfil the demands of the scene, the character must be seen to be…

The character's emotional state was revealed by…

[Character] wants…

The subtext of the character's lines is…

The audience is aware of the character's motivations through…

Analysing vocal skills

You might be required to write specifically about vocal techniques either as a named skill, such as 'use of voice', or within the broader term 'acting skills'.

Task C5

1 Experiment with saying the following line of dialogue:

> How dare you speak to me like that!

Try saying it in the following ways:
- As the queen, using a firm, commanding tone and an upper-class accent.
- As a fruit seller on a London market stall, when a customer has been rude to you. Use a Cockney accent, and increased volume.
- Shocked by what has been said, using a pause and a suprised tone.
- As a teenager joking around with a friend about something outrageous.

2 Write a paragraph describing in detail the vocal skills you used in part 1 of this task. Analyse what effects you hoped to achieve and evaluate the success of each of your choices.
- Which words did you emphasise?
- What was your tone of voice?
- What volume did you use?
- How did the use of accent affect how your character might be perceived?
- What emotion was expressed by your vocal choices?

3 Now try to remember three lines from a play you have seen, and describe, analyse and evaluate in detail how the lines were delivered.

TIP

It is very helpful when writing about vocal skills if you can quote a few lines or words from the play in order to provide precise examples of how vocal skills were used.

KEY TERM

Register: The vocal range of the voice (upper, middle or lower register) and the variety of tones of voice.

Useful vocabulary for discussing vocal skills

When writing about the vocal techniques performers have used, the words and phrases given here will be helpful.

Pitch
The vocal register used (high or low)

Pause
A hesitation or silence

Emotional range
The feelings expressed by the way lines are said

Intonation
The rise and fall of the voice in order to express meaning

Pace
How quickly or slowly the lines are spoken or sung

Emphasis
Stressing or highlighting particular words or phrases

Phrasing
How lines of dialogue are shaped, such as use of hesitation, rhythm, grouping certain words together

Accent
A way of pronouncing words that is associated with a particular country, region or social class

Volume
How loudly or quietly the lines are spoken or sung

Delivery
How lines are said in order to convey meaning

Task C6

Read the following response to a performance and annotate it with the vocal skills being discussed. Use the vocabulary given on the previous page.

As the music producer, the actor sounded a bit like the Rolling Stones singer Mick Jagger: he drawled certain words and used nasal elongated vowel sounds. This use of a slightly old-fashioned Cockney-type accent associated him with famous rock stars of the 1960s. ① He had excellent comic timing, saying some words very quickly, so that the audience couldn't help but be caught by surprise and laugh at some of his more outrageous lines. He would throw away lines like, 'a genius like me', showing how big his ego was. One scene that particularly showed the actor's skills was when he alternated between talking into his mobile phone and barking instructions at the singer. His use of two different tones was very noticeable, one which was softly intimate changing to one which was commanding and a bit frightening, especially when he said in a cold, matter-of-fact way, 'You're nothing without me.' The emphasis on the word 'nothing' was hard and cruel. This showed how the character was used to controlling people and being obeyed.

① Accent

TIP

If you can, quote two or three lines from the play you have seen in order to give precise examples of how vocal skills are used at a particular point.

Analysing physical skills

In the exam, you might be asked to write about physical skills, either as a named skilled, such as 'use of movement' or under the broader term 'acting skills'.

From the moment an actor appears on stage, you will begin assessing the character they are portraying based on the actor's physical skills, including their:

STANCE AND POSTURE
Straight or hunched, legs together or far apart...

FACIAL EXPRESSIONS
Relaxed or anxious, still or mobile, bland or expressive...

USE OF GESTURES
Powerful or apologetic, calm or frantic, repetitive or varied...

Task C7

1 Experiment with entering a room in different ways. Try out the following scenarios. Imagine you are:
   - A new student in a school and you have arrived late on the first day
   - An army general, getting ready to send your troops into battle
   - Rushing to see a good friend who has returned from a long trip
   - At a ceremony, walking onto a stage to receive a major award.

2 What physical skills did you use in each situation? Make notes on the following for each case:

Use of stage space
Did you use a lot of the space or confine yourself to a small section?

Gestures
Did you use any movements, such as waving to someone or nervously wringing your hands?

Facial expression
Did you smile or grimace? Did you attempt to make eye contact with anyone? Were you tense or relaxed?

Posture
Did you stand upright or were you bent over? Were you leading with a particular part of your body, for example your head, shoulders or feet?

Pace
How quickly or slowly did you move?

Task C8

Choose an entrance that you can remember from a play you have seen. Write about it in detail, noting similar points to those in the previous task.

Useful vocabulary for discussing physical skills

The following terms are useful for writing about performers' physical skills.

> **MOVEMENT**
> Changing positions or moving across an area

> **GESTURES**
> Small movements that tend to have meaning, such as hand or head movements

> **USE OF STAGE SPACE**
> How an actor moves around the stage

> **CHOREOGRAPHY**
> Setting movements to music to create dance or other movement sequences

> **POSTURE**
> The way a person stands

> **FACIAL EXPRESSIONS**
> Emotions (or lack of them) shown on a person's face

> **INTERACTION WITH OTHERS**
> How a character reacts to other characters, including movements, physical contact, body language and expressions

> **STAGE FIGHTS**
> Blocked movements to safely recreate violence on stage

> **GAIT**
> A way of walking

> **ENTRANCES AND EXITS**
> How an actor comes on stage or leaves it

> **HANDLING OF PROPS**
> Use of portable items, such as walking sticks, books, hand mirrors, brushes and so on

> **STAGE BUSINESS**
> Minor movements and/or blocking, such as tidying a room, reading a book or closing a window, in order to establish a situation.

Task C9

Read the performance response given below. Annotate it to show which physical acting skills are being discussed.

In the ghost scene, the actor portrayed both Hamlet and the ghost of his father. This involved very sophisticated use of physical skills. When playing the ghost, he would put on a large overcoat and change his posture, becoming very upright and rigid, ① seeming to grow before our eyes. He would use slow, powerful gestures, such as pointing where Hamlet had previously stood. He also made piercing eye contact with some members of the audience, suggesting his pain and the urgency of his demands. When becoming Hamlet again, the actor would throw off the coat and appear to shrink, his posture becoming hunched and his gestures tentative and fluttering. The transformation was accomplished very quickly, so that the audience was amazed by this virtuoso display of physical skills. At the end of the sequence, Hamlet collapsed to the floor as if exhausted.

① Posture

KEY TERM

Virtuoso: Highly skilled; expert in an artistic skill, such as music, dance or acting.

KEY TERMS

Describe: To give details of what you saw, heard or experienced.

Analyse: To examine something, perhaps by looking at the different elements of it, and to explain it.

Evaluate: To judge or form an opinion, such as explaining what effect was created and how successful it was.

Understanding an exam question about acting

The exact wording of the examination questions will vary from year to year, but you might be asked a question which resembles the one here. Use the notes to help you to think about the detail that will be required.

> **Describe** ① how **one or more actors** in a **particular section** ② of the play used their **acting skills** ③ to create **interesting characters**. ④ **Analyse** ⑤ and **evaluate how successful** ⑥ they were in **communicating** their character **to the audience**. ⑦

① Give precise examples so the examiner can picture what you mean.

② 'A particular section', unless otherwise specified, could refer to a single interlude or scene in a play, or could be a longer section, such as a full act. On the other hand, you might be guided to refer to the whole play or to key moments from the play.

③ Acting skills, unless specified, should include both vocal and physical skills.

④ Think about characterisation – instead of 'interesting', other possible wording could include 'believable', 'convincing', 'appropriate', 'effective', 'compelling' and so on.

⑤ To analyse, you need to examine in detail and break down the specific elements, such as use of volume or gesture.

⑥ Did the performers' choices and abilities, in your opinion, work for you and the rest of the audience?

⑦ What impact did the choices and techniques have on the audience and their understanding of the play? You might also be asked to consider how the characterisation contributed to the action, style or genre of the play.

Describing your production and choosing what to write about

It is unlikely that the examiner will have seen the production that you will be writing about. Therefore, your writing must describe the production clearly so that the examiners can understand what you are analysing and evaluating. Examiners are aware that different learning centres will be watching and learning about a variety of plays, so the question they include in the exam must be fairly general. It cannot specify which character or which section of the play you should write about, as the question must suit the wide range of productions seen. It is your responsibility, therefore, to choose a suitable character or characters and an appropriate section of the play about which to write.

◂ *Mimi Ndiweni as Ophelia with Paapa Essiedu as Hamlet, RSC*

Analysis and evaluation

Task C10

Read the following sample candidate-style responses and decide which one contains more analysis and evaluation.

> The actor playing Hamlet looked young, pale and thin. He spoke quickly, with a fairly low-pitched voice. Sometimes he would suddenly pause and look out at the audience. He would use gestures, such as grabbing the back of his neck. He was confident about using the whole stage area. He would move quickly from upstage to downstage or climb onto bits of stage furniture. He was very rough when he threw Ophelia to the ground.

> The actor's interpretation of Hamlet was a man on the verge of a nervous breakdown. This portrayal was reinforced by his use of vocal skills. At one moment, he would speak fluently and musically, but, in the scene with Ophelia, he appeared both to be 'feigning' madness but also truly distressed. The volume of his voice was at one moment soft and barely audible, then suddenly bursting with anger, such as when he shouted, 'Get thee to the nunnery.' The actor's vocal work was supported by his physical skills, including his hunched, defeated posture from which he would suddenly strike out angrily. His apparent lack of control kept the audience enthralled, wondering what he would do next.

Although the first response describes a number of useful acting skills, it does not analyse why the choices were made nor evaluate the success of them, beyond suggesting that the actor was 'confident'. In the second response, the details are more precise. Phrases such as 'the actor's interpretation' and 'he appears both to be...' suggest analysis, while 'kept the audience enthralled' is evaluative.

TIP

Remember that, in order to produce a high-quality response, it is important that you don't just describe what you have seen, but that you also analyse why the choices were made and evaluate the effect that they had.

Task C11

1 Write a paragraph describing the acting skills used by one of the actors in a performance you have seen. Then mark:
   - **D** for every description you provide
   - **A** for every analysis when you write about why and how effects were created
   - **E** for every evaluation when you write how successful it was.

2 Read through your paragraph. If you are lacking any of the key elements, rewrite it to make sure you have included examples of description, analysis and evaluation.

Zach Grenier and Lisa Emery in a Broadway production of Gabriel ▲

Choosing key moments from a performance

When discussing performance, you will need to choose which character or characters to write about and from which sections of the play. There is no one right way of doing this, but it is important that you choose a section or key moments that enable you to demonstrate your skills. Particularly interesting moments might be when:

▸ A character is introduced or undergoes a change

▸ A secret is revealed

▸ There is a moment of high emotion

▸ There is a technically difficult demand on the actor (such as a stage fight, multi-rolling, use of disguise or choreography).

An example of a key section: *Gabriel* by Moira Buffini

Gabriel is set on Guernsey in 1943 during the German occupation. Jeanne Becquet, an elegant Guernsey woman, goes out with a Nazi officer whom she believes can only speak German.

The grid below shows how you could begin to choose key moments from a section of a drama in order to analyse and evaluate acting skills.

Key moment	Effects to be achieved	Acting skills used	
Von Pfunz's entrance	Jeanne seems in control of the situation, while Von Pfunz appears comic and foolish	Von Pfunz	• Facial expressions: Open, smiling, not seeming to understand anything. • Gestures/posture: Gallant and formal, opening doors, trying to please.
		Jeanne	• Pace: Moves slowly, gracefully. • Facial expressions: Change between when she thinks Von Pfunz can see her and when she reveals her true feelings. She smiles at Von Pfunz's foolishness when he doesn't seem to understand.
Von Pfunz and Jeanne converse	• Establishing that Von Pfunz seems to speak only German, giving Jeanne freedom to say whatever she likes in English. • Audience will be surprised by how rude she is while pretending to be polite and welcoming.	Von Pfunz	• Accent: The very little English he speaks is highly accented and spoken in a stilted way like a schoolboy reading from a language book. • Pitch: High-pitched giggle, emphasises how comic he is. • Gesture: Wafts his hands, searching for words he seems not to know.
		Jeanne	• Intonation/delivery: The pleasant tone she uses when she speaks is in contrast with the insulting things she says. • Handling of props: Elegant use of cigarette case.
Revelation that Von Pfunz speaks perfect English	• A shock for both the audience and Jeanne that Von Pfunz has understood everything she said. • Changes from a comic scene to something serious and sinister.	Von Pfunz	• Facial expression: Drops open smile – instead looks slyly at Jeanne, with a satisfied grin. • Voice: Speaks perfect, if lightly accented, English. • Posture: Stands upright, assumes high status.
		Jeanne	• Handling of prop: Hides her shock by slowly taking a drink before responding. • Voice: Controls her voice to speak at a steady tempo.

Task C12

Use the format of the grid above to choose key moments from the play you have seen. Make sure that you have chosen a section with enough scope to discuss a variety of acting skills and effects.

Evaluating actors' performances

In order to produce a high-quality response to a question about performance, you will need to make insightful evaluative comments. In order to do this, you could consider:

▸ What were the actors trying to achieve in their performances?

▸ What impact did their acting skills have on the audience?

▸ How did the acting choices contribute to the meaning of the play?

▸ How did the choices contribute to the style of the play?

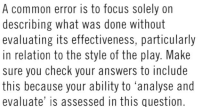
TIP

A common error is to focus solely on describing what was done without evaluating its effectiveness, particularly in relation to the style of the play. Make sure you check your answers to include this because your ability to 'analyse and evaluate' is assessed in this question.

What are the actors trying to achieve?

● Did they fulfil your expectations of the character, capturing their age, status, occupation and relationship with other characters?

● Did you, from their performance, feel you had an insight into what the character wanted and felt?

What impact did their acting skills have on the audience?

● Remember, you are an important audience member, so can write about your reactions, as well as those of people around you.

● If it was a comedy, did the audience smile or laugh at appropriate places?

● If it was a tragic piece, was the audience moved at the end?

● Was the audience engaged by the performances?

● Did anything surprise or shock the audience?

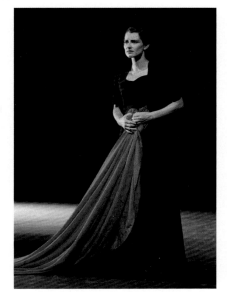

How did the acting choices contribute to the meaning of the play?

● Did they create characters who made sense within the period and setting of the play?

● Did they help you to understand the plot and message of the play?

How did the acting choices contribute to the style of the play?

● If it was a slapstick comedy, how did the acting choices add to the humour?

● If it was a highly naturalistic play, how believable were the performances?

● If there were complex movement sequences, were the performers able to deliver these in a slick, professional way?

Useful vocabulary for analysing performance

When writing about how an actor has used their skills, the words and phrases offered here will be helpful.

Making positive evaluative comments

Sentence starters such as these can help you to structure your writing:

▸ The actor contributed to the comedy/tragedy/drama of the piece by…
▸ This caused the audience to…
▸ From this performance, the audience understood…
▸ A powerful choice was…
▸ The actor fully inhabited the character by…
▸ The audience was moved by…
▸ The actor's physical skills made clear…
▸ The actor's use of voice suggested the character's emotions, such as…

Offering constructive criticism

You might see a production in which you feel a performance was disappointing or inadequate. As long as you can analyse why the performance was, in your opinion, unsuccessful, you can explain how you think it could have been improved.

▸ The actor did not fully realise the extreme emotions of the character and…
▸ The performance lacked the necessary…
▸ Although convincing in some sections, at this moment, the performer…
▸ The relationship between the lead characters was disappointing because…
▸ At this key moment, the reactions didn't seem believable because…
▸ Technically, the performance was flawed because… (perhaps it couldn't be heard/seen/understood or did not suit the style or context, for example).
▸ The actor was not well cast in the role because…

Task C13

1 Think of a performance that you were impressed by. Look at the following selection of positive evaluative words and then write a paragraph using at least three of them to discuss a performance you admired (or, if none of these words is appropriate, your own positive adjectives).

convincing comic varied surprising relatable mesmerising
thrilling skilful commanding charismatic consistent
frightening varied truthful enthralling

2 Think of a performance you have seen which you feel could have been improved. Look at the following selection of words and then write a paragraph using some of them in relation to the performance you are criticising (or use your own critical adjectives).

disappointing unconvincing over-exaggerated awkward
unbelievable limited stilted inaudible incomplete
monotonous shallow bland repetitive inappropriate
inexpressive unemotional

Analysing costume design, including hair and make-up

When writing about the costumes you have seen, you could consider:

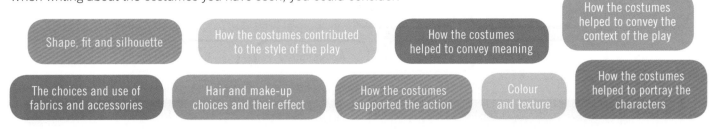

Shape, fit and silhouette

How the costumes contributed to the style of the play

How the costumes helped to convey meaning

How the costumes helped to convey the context of the play

The choices and use of fabrics and accessories

Hair and make-up choices and their effect

How the costumes supported the action

Colour and texture

How the costumes helped to portray the characters

In order to prepare for this, it is important to make detailed notes shortly after seeing the production, so that you don't forget vital details. Photographs are also helpful to remind you of details. You can also make additional notes on them during revision.

This photograph is from *The Visit* at the Williamstown Festival Theatre, starring Chita Rivera as Claire Zachanassian. The costume designer was Ann Hould Ward.

> **KEY TERMS**
>
> **Entourage:** A group of people who escort or assist an important person.
>
> **Tragicomic:** A creative work, such as a play or novel, with both tragic and comic elements.

Context: Design suggests an earlier time and fur on clothing suggests a cold location.

Hat: White fur.

Hair: Dark, which contrasts with paleness of face and white outfit. Heavily styled.

Make-up: Pale face, drawing attention to eyes and lips. Bright red lipstick is vivid and suggests an earlier period. Possibly makes her look cruel.

Condition and fit of outfit: As if new and fitting perfectly.

Accessories: Expensive-looking jewellery including 'diamonds' and 'rubies' (indicates wealth).

Long white gloves: Gives a sense of old-fashioned formality and perhaps attendance at an exclusive event.

Walking stick: Suggests age, frailty.

Sunglasses and white sticks for the entourage: suggesting they are blind.

Colour palette: Mostly contrasting black and white, with striking yellow highlights. White for Claire, which makes her stand out from her entourage and the dark set. The only use of pattern is in the necklace.

Coat: Full length, off-white, silk-type material, with fur collar and cuffs.

Fabric: Fur (fake for costume, but appears genuine: expensive).

Texture: Smooth fabric, complemented with soft, fluffy 'fur'.

Dress: Full length white, empire-line with low bodice, bow detail.

Silhouette: Long coat, suggests late 19th or early 20th century.

Stylised use of highlights, such as yellow platform shoes and the white make-up for two of the characters, suggests a heightened style rather than realism and creates an eerie effect suited to the tragicomic style and message.

Task C14

Look at the photographs below and annotate them with as many points as you can about:

(Fabric) (Colours) (Texture) (Silhouette) (Make-up)

(Style) (Context) (Hair) (Accessories) (Condition and fit)

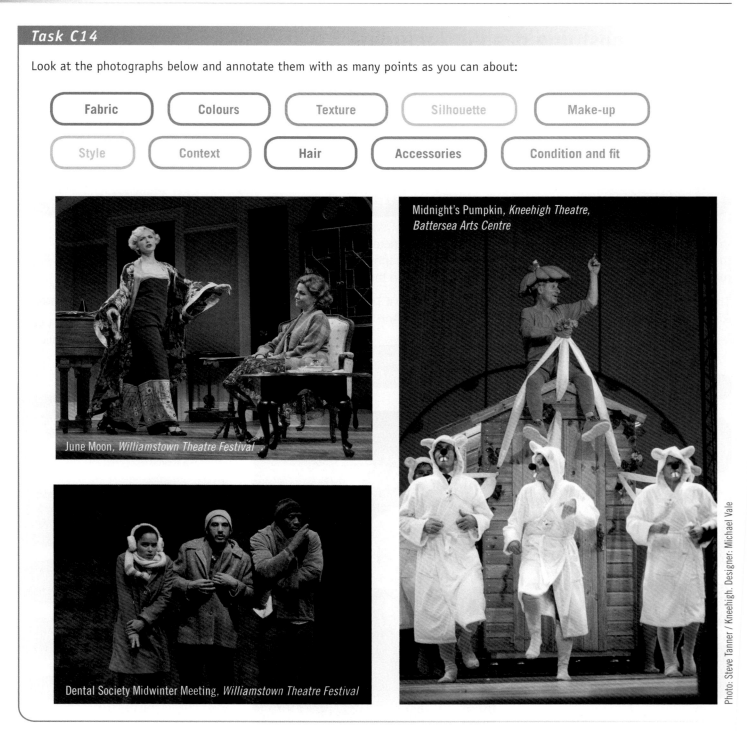

June Moon, Williamstown Theatre Festival

Dental Society Midwinter Meeting, Williamstown Theatre Festival

Midnight's Pumpkin, Kneehigh Theatre, Battersea Arts Centre

Photo: Steve Tanner / Kneehigh. Designer: Michael Vale

Task C15

Sketch an outline figure and draw in as much detail as you can of a costume you have seen in a play. Annotate it with its various design features as listed in the word bank above.

How costumes contribute to a play's action, style and context

Costumes are not merely decorative additions to a production. The audience expects to be able to 'read' a character partly by what they wear and how they look, and to use the costumes to better understand the play's setting, context and style.

A common error for students in exams is simply to describe costumes rather than analysing how they contribute to the play or evaluating how successful they were.

Task C16

Read the following two responses to the costumes in *The Visit* (shown on page 107). Note any examples of:

- Description (D)
- Analysis (A)
- Evaluation (E).

An example of each has been included for you.

> As Claire is returning to the town for revenge, the designer has created costumes which emphasise her wealth. Ⓐ The costume designer, Ann Hould Ward, has dressed Claire entirely in white, which contrasts both with the dark colours worn by her male entourage, but also with the poor clothes of the inhabitants of the town. Her clothes fit perfectly and are in pristine condition – highlighted by their shiny, spotless whiteness, whereas the townspeople's costumes are dull, shabby, mended and loose-fitting. Ⓓ The fabrics used further emphasise her wealth – the white coat suggests the finest silk, while the trim is fur, such as might be found on an Arctic fox. When she is on stage, it is impossible to take your eyes off Claire, which is surely the effect the designer wanted.

> The style of the production is tragicomic and, at times, expressionistic. It is also a musical, so the costumes have been designed so that the performers can move easily in them. Rivera, as Claire, can remove the coat, so that the empire line flowing dress underneath allows for more movement and gives her a more fluent silhouette. The blinded entourage figures are both eerie and comic. They are dressed identically to emphasise that they work as a team. Their outfits combine conventional black suits and bowler hats with stylistic effects, such as the white-face masks and yellow shoes. The effect is to remove any sense of their individuality. This succeeds Ⓔ in making the audience accept Claire's cruelty more easily.

Task C17

1 Write one paragraph about one or more costumes in a play you have seen. Explain how the costumes support the play's style, plot and/or context.

2 Afterwards, read your work to check that you have included description, analysis and evaluation.

 TIP

There is no one 'right' answer to this question. Both of the sample responses here are strong, although they make different points about the costumes in *The Visit*.

KEY TERMS

Pristine: As if new; perfect; clean.

Expressionistic: A non-naturalistic style that highlights subjective emotions.

Deciding what to write about costumes

You might see a production in which there are dozens of exciting costumes that you could write about. Avoid the temptation to try to write about them all. In the time you have available in the exam, it is far better to write in detail about a limited number of costumes.

The grid below offers one way to make notes about costumes. Once you have completed a grid like this for the show you have seen, you will find it easier to select those costumes about which you have the most to say.

 **CHECK IT OUT**

Page 178 of *AQA GCSE Drama* has more samples of student-style responses on costume design.

 TIP

Remember to consider if a costume is changed or altered in the course of the play. What are the effects of the changes?

Detailed costume description	What the costume communicates about character, plot, style and context	How the costume is used in the play	How effective it is
• Naturalistic period costume. • Secretary's costume: – 1930s navy blue dress. White collar, high neckline. Below the knee. Light wool fabric. – Matching coat, with belt. – Cloche hat. – Low-heeled strap shoes. – Simple necklace and small gold earrings.	• The character is prim and proper, contrasting with the more flamboyant wife, who usually wears red. • The period is reflected in the style of dress and fabric used, as well as the distinctive hat: the style is clearly early 20th century.	• The character puts on a hat and coat when she vows to leave her boss. • The low-heeled leather shoes fit her practical personality, but also make it possible for the actor to perform the choreography.	The outfit was partially successful. It perhaps looked a little too worn and dowdy in the office scenes, considering she is meant to be a love rival to the wife, but the transformation when she put on the hat and coat were effective – she suddenly looked like an interesting, independent businesswoman in her own right.
• Stylised modern costume. • Cardboard was used in many costumes, including being taped on the soldiers to serve as armour or shaped into large rigid skirts for the women. These items were placed over the loose grey cotton trousers and T-shirts they otherwise were wearing.	• The play was set in a refugee camp where the performers appeared to use the resources around them to create costumes. • Besides cardboard, other materials, all made from easily available items, included: – Gaffer tape – Crayons to add decoration and colour – Black bin bags for draping – Tin cans.	There were short interludes when characters would be seen on stage fashioning a costume on others, leading to the performer gradually acquiring the costume that suited their character.	Using 'found' items to create the costumes was continually interesting and creative. The queen's costume was particularly successful. It involved a pleated cardboard skirt, a draped bin-liner bodice and a crown fashioned from a tin can. She seemed to be at once a refugee and a proud queen.

Useful vocabulary for describing and discussing costumes

When writing about the details of costumes, including headwear, hairstyles and make-up, you should find the following words and phrases helpful.

Fabric

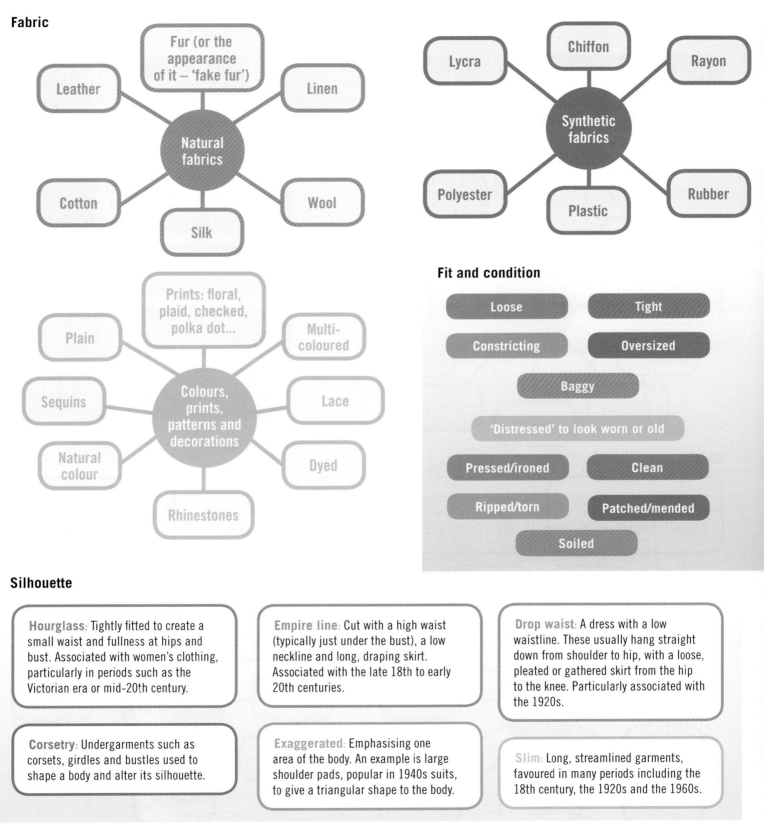

Silhouette

Hourglass: Tightly fitted to create a small waist and fullness at hips and bust. Associated with women's clothing, particularly in periods such as the Victorian era or mid-20th century.

Empire line: Cut with a high waist (typically just under the bust), a low neckline and long, draping skirt. Associated with the late 18th to early 20th centuries.

Drop waist: A dress with a low waistline. These usually hang straight down from shoulder to hip, with a loose, pleated or gathered skirt from the hip to the knee. Particularly associated with the 1920s.

Corsetry: Undergarments such as corsets, girdles and bustles used to shape a body and alter its silhouette.

Exaggerated: Emphasising one area of the body. An example is large shoulder pads, popular in 1940s suits, to give a triangular shape to the body.

Slim: Long, streamlined garments, favoured in many periods including the 18th century, the 1920s and the 1960s.

Colour

Colour palette: The range of colours used. For example, a limited palette would only include a few colours.

Colour coding: Using colours to indicate something about characters, such as a family group or to suggest a character's transition by moving from muted tones to bright colours.

Padding

Protective padding: Clothing with extra cushioning to protect performers in difficult or dangerous physical tasks.

Shoulder padding: Pads or extra material at the shoulders to create a broad-shouldered silhouette.

Character padding: To add weight to or change the shape of a character, such as with a 'pregnancy belly' or 'humpback'.

Footwear

Decorative details

Buttons: Size, colour, plain or decorative.

Embroidery: Decorative stitching.

Braid: Woven cord or other fabrics, such a gold braid added to a jacket.

Trim: Additional decorative items, such as fur on the collar or cuffs of a jacket or a fringe on a skirt.

Style

Period/historical: Designed to replicate or suggest a particular time period.

Fantastical/stylised: Designed to suggest non-naturalistic characters or situations, such as representing animals, inanimate objects or futuristic, exaggerated, abstract or symbolic figures.

Modern/contemporary: Representing current fashions and trends.

Hats

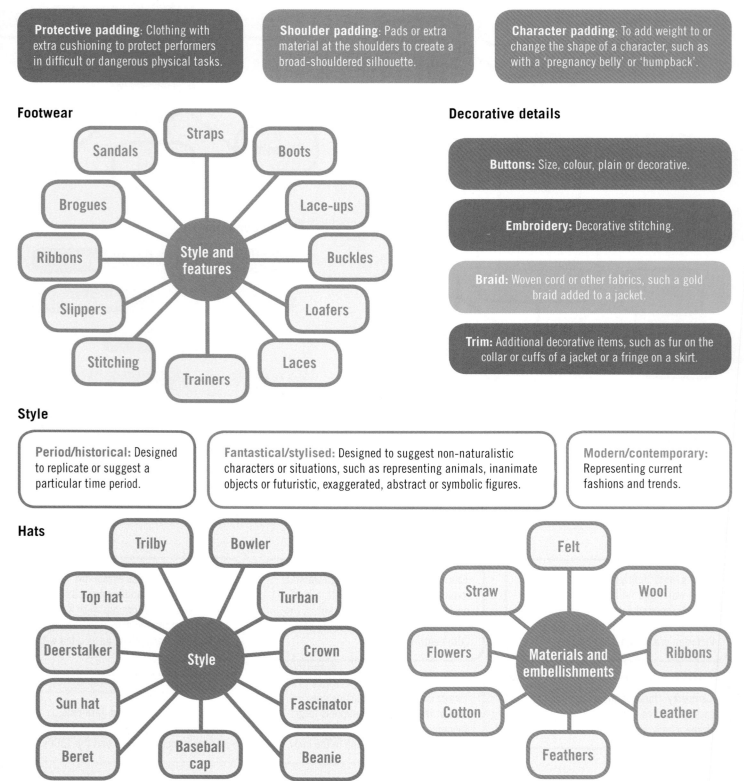

Hair

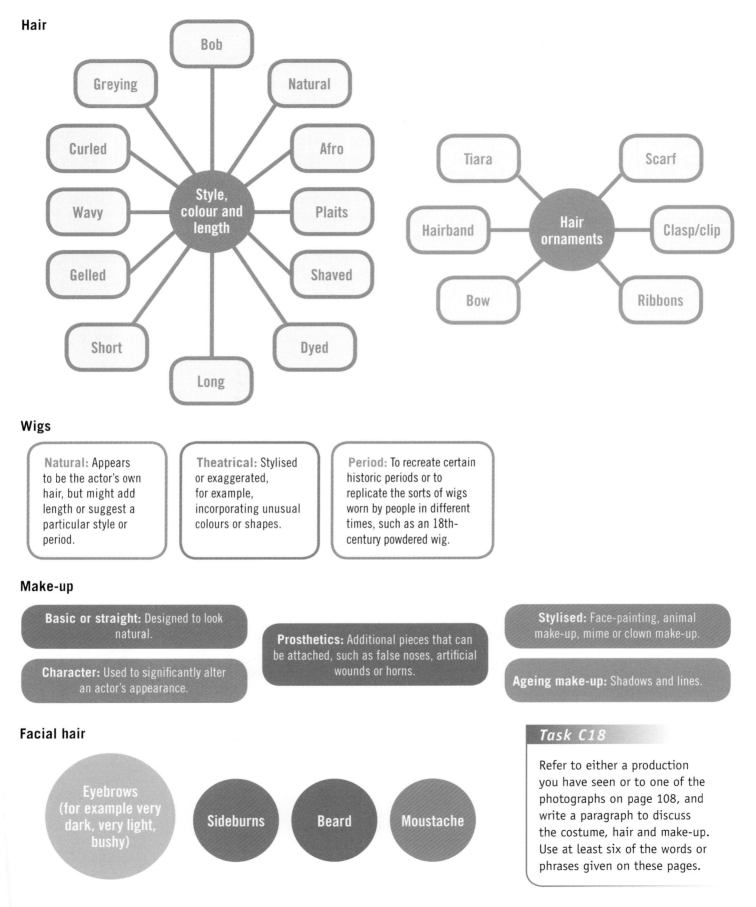

Style, colour and length
- Bob
- Natural
- Greying
- Curled
- Afro
- Wavy
- Plaits
- Gelled
- Shaved
- Short
- Dyed
- Long

Hair ornaments
- Tiara
- Scarf
- Hairband
- Clasp/clip
- Bow
- Ribbons

Wigs

Natural: Appears to be the actor's own hair, but might add length or suggest a particular style or period.

Theatrical: Stylised or exaggerated, for example, incorporating unusual colours or shapes.

Period: To recreate certain historic periods or to replicate the sorts of wigs worn by people in different times, such as an 18th-century powdered wig.

Make-up

Basic or straight: Designed to look natural.

Character: Used to significantly alter an actor's appearance.

Prosthetics: Additional pieces that can be attached, such as false noses, artificial wounds or horns.

Stylised: Face-painting, animal make-up, mime or clown make-up.

Ageing make-up: Shadows and lines.

Facial hair

- Eyebrows (for example very dark, very light, bushy)
- Sideburns
- Beard
- Moustache

Task C18

Refer to either a production you have seen or to one of the photographs on page 108, and write a paragraph to discuss the costume, hair and make-up. Use at least six of the words or phrases given on these pages.

Analysing set design

When writing about the set and prop design of the play you have seen, consider:

▸ How the set helped to communicate meaning
▸ How the set contributed to the style of the play
▸ What the set and props conveyed about the characters and context
▸ How the set and props helped the action
▸ How the set and props contributed to mood or atmosphere
▸ The staging configuration
▸ Any essential or particularly interesting furnishings, dressings and props
▸ The colours, textures and materials used in the set
▸ Any backdrops, flats or projections
▸ Whether one set was used or if there were set changes or a composite set
▸ Any levels, ramps or staircases
▸ Where entrances and exits occurred.

The photograph on the following page shows a scene from a 2013 production of *Pygmalion*, designed by Alexander Dodge and set in the early 20th century.

Task C19

After studying the *Pygmalion* set and its accompanying annotations, answer the following questions.

1 How does the set convey the period of the play?
2 What does the set suggest about the character who owns this room, Henry Higgins? What are likely to be his interests, his social position and his personality?
3 What effect do you think this set would have on the audience? Would they be impressed by it? Interested in what happens in this space? Curious about the characters who live in this space?

TIP

There will be three options for Section C in the exam. If one of the questions is about set design, it could be something like the following.

'Describe how the set was used to help the audience understand the style and action of the play.

Analyse and evaluate how successful they were in creating an interesting and effective set.'

You might want to write about:

● The use of space, levels and scale
● Colours, textures and materials.

Remember that the question will be worth 32 marks.

LOOK HERE

See pages 127 and 135–137 for more Section C exam-type questions.

A traditional period set for *Pygmalion*

Fabrics: Leather sofa, wooden furniture, wool carpet

Set dressings: Portraits, art, books

Floor covering: Geometric-patterned, yellow-toned carpet

Stage furnishings: Small leather sofa centre stage. Small table and two wooden chairs stage right. Cushioned footstool stage left. Wooden chair stage left. Desk and chair upstage centre. Cabinets along upstage wall.

Wall coverings: Elaborate, bold leaf-pattern, period wallpaper

Set changes: Five acts in the play involve five set changes, including an outdoor scene in Covent Garden, Mrs Higgins' drawing room and this set of Professor Higgins' study.

Staging configuration: End on

Texture: Most surfaces are smooth. Room appears clean but cluttered

Levels: Small staircase/ladder leading to pipe organ on upper platform

Context: Edwardian period

Entrances/exits: Five doors: one upstage right, two stage right and two stage left

Style of set: Naturalistic, box set

Colours: Green, white and purple wallpaper. Yellow and blue carpet. Light- and mid-brown wood

A modern set in *For the Lulz*

Below is a modern, minimalist set for a play called *For the Lulz* about a computer hacker who attacks social networks.

Set changes: One set is used to suggest several different locations, with stage furnishing, such as a desk, brought on and off as necessary.

Colours: Dark, with black floor and background, as well as black chairs. The red and green design on the floor breaks up the darkness.

Staging configuration: Thrust

Style: Minimalistic, non-naturalistic

Context: Modern, contemporary

Backdrop/flats: Black flat with projections

Floor coverings: Black floor with green lines (tape) and red dots. Geometric appearance. Might suggest the workings of the Internet.

Entrances/exits: Can occur through audience or from upstage. No practical doors appear in the set.

Stage furnishings: Black office chair on castors, laptop

KEY TERM

Minimalist: Simple, spare; using few elements; stripped back.

Task C20

Read the annotations around the photograph and then answer these questions.

1 How does the set design reinforce the issues of hacking and social media explored in the play?
2 How can the audience tell from the design that this is a modern play discussing contemporary issues?
3 What mood or atmosphere is established by the set?
4 What aspects of the set design do you think might intrigue the audience?

An expansive outdoor set for *Lord of the Flies*

Task C21

Look closely at this photograph of an outdoor production of *Lord of the Flies* at Regent's Park Open Air Theatre, designed by Jon Bausor.

Make detailed notes, similar to those around the photographs on the previous pages, about its set design.

Task C22

Draw a detailed sketch of the set in the production you watched. If it had any complete set changes, draw separate sketches to show each complete set.

On your sketches, note:
- Staging configuration
- Colours, fabrics and textures used
- Any stage furnishings and props
- How scene changes occurred
- Levels, entrances and exits.

CHECK IT OUT

See pages 179–180 of *AQA GCSE Drama* for more ideas about analysing and evaluating sets.

How set design contributes to action, style and context

Many theatrical productions do not use curtains, so audiences might see some or all of the set when they first walk into the auditorium. You might, therefore, have an instant impression of the production you are going to see and you might begin to make judgements about it. You could see a play with an expensive, complex set or a simpler minimalistic set or a single naturalistic set. Whatever play you see, you must be able to identify the choices the set designer has made and how they help to convey the play's meaning.

TIP

A common error in the exam is simply to describe the set design rather than analysing how it contributes to the play or evaluating how successful it was. Remember to include analysis and evaluation.

Task C23

Read the following samples of candidate-style responses about two set designs for two different productions. Note any examples of:

- Description (D)   • Analysis (A)   • Evaluation (E).

Ⓓ Description of style.

> The set of <u>Summer and Smoke</u>, designed by Tom Scutt, was not the naturalistic type of set many associate with the work of playwright Tennessee Williams. Instead, the design was minimalistic Ⓓ and stripped back, showing the bare brick walls of the theatre and a plain floor. Two steps up from the main acting area was a semi-circle of nine pianos around the acting space. These pianos were used by the actors to create music, but also to represent Alma's love of the arts. This choice was highly effective because it removed the clutter which often accompanies naturalistic plays and put the focus on the characters, particularly Alma. The pianos also added excitement to the staging, as actors would perch on top or walk across them or sit down to play them, creating a soundtrack.

Ⓐ Analysis of what the set had to achieve.

Task C24

Consider the set for a production you have seen and write a paragraph about how it was used to support the play's style, context and action. Afterwards, check over your work, making sure you have described (D), analysed (A) and evaluated (E).

> The set of <u>Sunset Boulevard</u> recreated Hollywood of the early 20th century. The designer had the difficult task of creating a range of complex sets which had to be moved quickly into place to suggest new locations. Ⓐ Also, as this was a touring production, the set had to fit a wide range of theatres. Norma Desmond's house, with its grand staircase and yellow velvet sofa suggested an earlier era which contrasted with the bright casual diner set where the studio workers met and partied. This made clear the choice Joe would have to make – the dark past with Norma or the bright future with Betty. One element of the design which divided opinion was the use of an incomplete prop-type car. While some didn't like it as it distanced them from the impending tragedy, I felt it worked well because it reflected Norma's inability to separate fantasy from reality. The use of projected films, including Norma as a young girl, was also successful as it reinforced the play's preoccupation with film-making and the distance between Norma as a young woman and how she now appeared.

Useful vocabulary for discussing set design

Using technical terminology correctly will help you to produce high-quality writing. It is unlikely that the production you will see will use all of the following, but see if any can be included in your practice writing about set design.

Backdrop
A large painted cloth hung as part of the scenery.

Cyclorama
A large semi-circular stretched curtain or screen, usually positioned upstage. This is often used to depict a background, such as the sky.

Drapes
Curtains or other hanging fabric.

Flat
A piece of scenery mounted on a frame.

Furnishings
Furniture on the set, such as chairs, cushions and tables.

Fly system
A means of raising and lowering scenery or other items onto the stage using a system of ropes and pulleys. You can refer to 'flying a set in'.

Multimedia
Use of film or other media during the production.

Revolve
A large turntable device that can be turned to reveal a different setting.

Projection
Projecting a film or still image to form a theatrical backdrop.

Symbolic
Using something to represent something else. A symbolic stage set might be a non-naturalistic design to suggest something about the play and its themes, such as a heavy use of red to suggest violence, or a house wall with a crack down its middle to suggest a family torn apart.

Scrims
Gauze stage curtains which, depending how they are lit, can either be opaque or translucent.

Set dressings
Items on the set not actually used as props, but that create detail and interest, such as vases or framed paintings.

Trapdoor
A door in the floor of a stage allowing objects or performers to be dropped, lifted or lowered.

Truck
A platform on wheels upon which scenery can be mounted and moved.

Wing space
An area to the side of the stage from which actors can enter and from which props, furnishings or sets can be moved onto the stage.

Task C25

Check your notes on the production you have seen and highlight any of the terms above that could be used to explain and discuss in a technically accurate way what you have seen.

Analysing lighting design

Below is an example of stage lighting from the Company One production of *Shockheaded Peter*.

Floor lights and footlights used to create uplighting and shadows.

Low intensity wash of light on stage keeps all figures lit to some degree.

Red filter used (particularly seen on central figure's forehead).

Shadows on back wall create eerie, frightening effect.

Two figures in the foreground are lit with the most intensity.

Uplighting casts shadows on faces, particularly under eyes of central figure.

Footlights contribute to Victorian period and music-hall feel of the design.

A different use of lighting is seen in *The Old Man and the Old Moon* from PigPen Theatre Company who use storytelling techniques in their plays.

Intense backlighting used to create shadow puppet effect.

Sections of the stage in darkness.

Sources of lighting are not hidden, but are part of the performance.

Performer also uses portable handheld light.

Lighting colours: golden yellow.

Uplighting, probably from a floor light, casts light on the storyteller's face.

Task C26

Make detailed notes about the lighting in a production you have seen, including:

- Is lighting subtle or noticeable?
- How are transitions handled? Are there blackouts? Fades? Cross-fades?
- Are the sources of light visible or hidden?
- What colours of lighting are used?
- Are there any special effects created by lighting?
- Is there any particular focusing of light, on a face or prop, for example?
- Can you see examples of different uses of light?
- How are the lighting effects created, do you think?
- Are there key moments when lighting is used particularly noticeably or effectively?

Choosing key moments where lighting is important

Use a grid like the one below to select key lighting states and transitions and to evaluate how effective they were in the production you watched.

Lighting state/transition	Description	Evaluation
At the opening of the play, a sunlit drawing room in an English country house	<ul><li>House lights dim and stage lights fade up to reveal room.</li><li>Golden/orange light, probably from a fresnel lantern in the wings, angled down to recreate effect of light streaming through the window.</li><li>General wash of light in the rest of the room.</li><li>Midway through the scene, an actor 'turns on' a desk lamp.</li><li>Gradual fade down of window and general wash lights at the end of the scene.</li></ul>	<ul><li>The lighting is successful in recreating a naturalistic English country setting, with the attractive light adding to the feeling of wealth and comfort of the family.</li><li>The use of onstage, visible lighting, such as the desk lamp appearing to be operated by actors, adds to the naturalism. This also highlights that it is getting late.</li></ul>
Transition between scenes	Between each episode of the play, two very bright tubes of light attached to two screens would appear. The shape of the lights had the appearance of fluorescent lamps, but, given their intensity, were probably LED lights. The tubes would suddenly flash, almost blinding the audience.	The effect was very disorienting. You could see the audience was shocked and made uncomfortable by the bright light. The technique signalled a sharp ending to each scene and meant that the audience's identification with the emotion of the previous scene was cut off before the next scene began.

CHECK IT OUT

See pages 182–183 of *AQA GCSE Drama* for more examples of lighting analysis and evaluation.

A fresnel lantern with barn doors ▲

KEY TERMS

Barn doors: Metal flaps used on fresnel lanterns to shape the light beam into, for example, a square. They also lessen the 'spill' of light, ensuring that a precise area is lit.

Pinspot: A spotlight so tightly focused it only lights a very small area.

Strobe: A lighting device that produces short bursts of light.

Task C28

Write two paragraphs about the lighting design in a production you have seen. Look over what you have written and mark examples of description, analysis and evaluation. If any are missing, go back and edit. Try to include some of the terms given on the following page.

How lighting contributes to a play's action, style and context

Your writing about lighting in live theatre should show that you understand how lighting contributed to the overall production. The lighting demands of a big musical, for example, will be very different from that of an intimate, minimalistic play. Some designs might simply indicate the beginning and end of scenes or the time of day; while others will have a wide variety of special effects.

Task C27

Read the following samples of candidate-style responses about two lighting designs. Note any examples of:

* Description (D)
* Analysis (A)
* Evaluation (E).

The lighting had an important role to play. The set was minimalistic, so the lighting established the location, time of day and mood of each scene. Instead of employing a general wash of light across the stage, the designer used a combination of profile and fresnel lanterns to focus attention on particular areas of the stage. Barn doors were used on the fresnel lanterns to restrict the spill of light and shape the illumination into tight rectangles, which suggested the claustrophobia of the cabin's rooms. The lighting added to the mystery and tension of the play, as you never knew where you would need to look next. (A) One particularly effective section was the scene when a gentle white light streamed in diagonally from upstage left to suggest the light from a kitchen window as a woman washed dishes. The mood was calm. Then, suddenly, a pinspot high-intensity green light snapped onto a strange woman's face outside the window, which made us jump with surprise.

Colour was important in this lighting design. This was particularly noticeable in the fight scene when red filters were introduced and increased in intensity and brightness as the gangs approached each other. When the physical altercation occurred, a strobe was employed. The effect was to plant a series of suspenseful still images in the audience's mind which occurred so quickly we could barely take them in. There would be a flash of light and we would see the group in a huddle, with Joe's arm outstretched. The next flash revealed a knife. Another showed the group pulling away from the centre. The last revealed Joe, apparently dead, on the ground centre stage, in the pool of an intense white spotlight beaming directly down from the lighting rig in the flies. Although it was undoubtedly an exciting use of light, I felt that using red to show violence was a little clichéd, but judging by the audience silence at the end of the sequence, it was clearly effective for others.

Useful vocabulary for discussing lighting design

Backlight
Light projected from a source upstage. It highlights the outline of actors or scenery and separates them from the background. It can also create sculptural effects.

Barn doors
Metal flaps used on fresnel lanterns to make the beam into a particular shape, such as a square. They also lessen the 'spill' of light.

Blackout
Switching off all stage lights. This can be sudden or gradual.

Black hole
An area of the stage accidentally left unlit.

Colour filter
Coloured pieces of plastic on a lantern that alter the colour of the light. Also called 'gels'.

Cross-fade
A transition in which lighting states are changed by bringing up the new state while reducing the old state.

Fade
To gradually bring up (fade up) or diminish lights (fade down).

Floodlight
A lantern without a lens, which produces an unfocused wash of light.

Floor lights
Lanterns on low stands, often used to cast shadows.

Fluorescent
Tubular lights used to efficiently and inexpensively light large areas. (Frequently used in schools, warehouses and factories.)

Focus
How tightly or sharply defined a beam of light is, such as a well-focused circle or square.

Followspot
A powerful spotlight operated so that its beam follows an actor around the stage.

Footlights
Low lights placed on the downstage front edge of the stage. These were popular in Victorian theatre and musical halls and are sometimes used to create period lighting effects.

TIP

A common exam error is simply to describe the lighting design. Remember to analyse how it contributed to the play and evaluate how successful it was.

Fresnel
A lantern with a lens that produces a soft-edged beam of light.

Gobo
A metal cut-out used to project patterns, such as leaves, stars, swirls or waves.

House lights
The lights in the auditorium that are usually on while the audience is being seated and then turned off as the performance is about to begin.

LED stage lighting
LED stands for 'light-emitting diode'. LEDs can be very powerful and colourful (without using gels) and are energy-efficient. They are unable, however, to create some effects used in traditional stage lighting, such as hard-edged beams.

Neon
Bright gas-filled tubes of light that are frequently used in electric signs.

Pinspot
A spotlight so tightly focused it only lights a very small area, such as a single object or an actor's face.

Profile
A type of lantern with a lens that can project clear outlines.

Smoke or haze machine
A machine that produces clouds or mist.

Strobe
A lighting device that gives short bursts of lighting.

Wash
Lighting that covers the whole stage.

Analysing sound design

When writing about sound design you might consider:

▶ Whether the sound design was naturalistic or abstract
▶ How the sound design contributed to the style of the play
▶ If sound contributed to the plot and action of the play
▶ If the sound design clarified the context or location of the play
▶ How sound helped to create certain moods or atmosphere
▶ How sound effects were accomplished
▶ If sound was amplified or distorted
▶ Whether sound effects were live or recorded
▶ What music was used
▶ If the use of sound affected the action on stage, such as actors moving in time with music
▶ Whether the sounds had an impact on the audience. Did the audience react to any sounds? Did the use of sound create tension or humour?

You might see a production which has sound and music at its heart. *The Dixon Family Album*, below, for example, uses actor-musicians to trace the fortunes of a folk music group in the 1960s.

Context: 1960s folk music, reinforces setting.

Singing: Actors sing on stage.

Actor-musicians: Instruments played live on stage.

Microphones: General-use microphones on stands to amplify singing and musical instruments.

Off stage: Drummer and additional sound equipment offstage left.

Some productions will make particular demands upon a sound designer, for example, if they occur in unusual places, such as outdoors, where the acoustics might be difficult. In the scene shown on the following page, from *Gigi* at Regent's Park Open Air Theatre, the performers are singing, and dancing to music, which contributes to the cheerful mood of the scene. Consider, however, how the outdoor setting means that speakers and microphones must be carefully placed and used, and that sound balancing can be difficult.

On the other hand, you might have seen a production which uses music in a subtle way, subliminally affecting the audience's mood. Or you might have seen a production in which naturalistic sound effects are important for the plot, such as gunshots, animal noises, crowds, traffic or alarms.

Task C29

Make detailed notes on the sound design of the production you have seen, using the bullet points on the previous page.

Choosing key moments of the use of sound

Use a grid like the one below to help you to select a suitable section of the production you have seen in order to describe, analyse and evaluate the sound design effectively.

Description of sound	Analysis of how it was achieved	Evaluation of its effect and impact
The sound of a slow metronome as the characters waited for the jury's verdict	This sound was recorded and then amplified on speakers that surrounded the stage. It snapped on and off.	The tick of the metronome was used to emphasise the tension of the long wait for judgement. It played for at least a minute, but seemed longer, especially as there was no other sound, creating significant tension for the audience and a sense of surprise when it suddenly stopped.

 TIP

If you choose to write about sound design for this section, you must ensure that you have seen a production that offers sufficient scope for you to be able to write thoroughly about the design. If you have seen a production with only one sound effect or a couple of minor music cues, you might find it difficult to write enough.

 **CHECK IT OUT**

See page 181 of *AQA GCSE Drama* for more advice on how to analyse and evaluate sound.

TIP

A common error in the exam is just to describe the sound design. Remember to include analysis of how it contributed to the play and evaluation of how successful it was.

How sound design contributes to action, style and context

Your writing about sound design in live theatre should show that you understand how sound contributes to the overall production. The sound demands of a big musical with a specially composed score and large orchestra, for example, will be very different from that of an intimate, minimalistic play with a few recorded sound effects. The use of sound might include effects created on stage, recorded sound effects or original music composition.

Task C30

Read the following samples of candidate-style responses about sound design in two different productions. Note any examples of:

- Description (D)
- Analysis (A)
- Evaluation (E).

Ⓓ Description of how sound assists the style of the play

In this production of <u>The Caucasian Chalk Circle</u> by Bertolt Brecht, the sound designer used sound to contribute to the epic style of the play. Ⓓ Brecht believed that the audience should not think they are watching real-life and used the alienation effect to remind them they were in a theatre watching actors. The sound design supported this, by showing the actors setting up microphone stands and testing microphones as the audience came in. In the scene by the river, an actor placed a general-use microphone on a low stand next to a bowl of water and created the splashing noises next to the actors enacting the scene. This added to the artificiality of the play's style. Additionally, all the actors played instruments (guitar, drums, tambourine, violin) and sang music which had been specially composed for this performance. This was always done in view of the audience, with the musicians either at the centre of the action or sitting downstage, watching the action. The music was more modern (rock rather than folk) and relevant to the audience than the style more usually associated with Brecht's plays.

KEY TERMS

Epic: A type of early 20th-century theatre particularly associated with Bertolt Brecht. It is non-naturalistic and uses particular techniques to remind the audience they are watching a play.

Alienation effect: A distancing effect that prevents the audience from believing they are watching a real event. It might involve breaking the fourth wall by speaking directly to the audience or drawing attention to the mechanics behind the play's production.

Task continued on next page

In this play, set in an Internet chatroom, music played a vital role. (A) The audience was immediately startled when the characters entered to a recording of the Oompa Loompa song from the 1971 Willy Wonka film. The volume was loud, with speakers at the front of the stage blasting the song out as the actors, dressed in ordinary contemporary clothes, but moving rigidly in time with the music, entered. The effect was odd, making the audience laugh and preparing them for a play which would surprise them repeatedly. The song snapped off and the actors seamlessly began their dialogue. To reinforce the setting, the sound design incorporated a range of recorded notification 'pings' and 'whoosh' sound effects to punctuate the characters' online debates. At the end of the first scene, there was loud burst of Prodigy's 'Firestarter' song, approximately 20 seconds, which accompanied the actors' 'chairography' as they positioned the chairs for the next scene. This use of sound and music made the production seem modern and relevant, as well as keeping the pace high. Additionally, the choice of 'Firestarter' added a sense of danger.

(A) Analysis of how important sound was to establishing the location and period of the play

KEY TERM

Chairography: Choreographed movement involving moving or rearranging chairs on the stage.

Task C31

Consider this exam-style question:

'Describe how sound was used in the production to create mood and/or atmosphere. Analyse and evaluate how successful the sound design was in affecting the audience's experience and understanding of the play. You could make reference to:

- The use of sound effects and music, including any special techniques
- How and at what level the sound is projected and amplified
- A notable section of the play or the play as a whole.'

In response, write two paragraphs about the sound design for a section of the play you have seen. Afterwards, go over your writing, noting when you have:

- Described (D)
- Analysed (A)
- Evaluated (E).

If you are missing any of these, rewrite the paragraphs to make sure you can include them.

Useful vocabulary for discussing sound design

Abstract
Symbolic, not realistic, such as a loud beating heart for tension or dripping water to suggest the passing of time.

Actor-musicians
Performers who play musical instruments as part of their acting roles.

Acoustics
The sound quality in a space, such as whether an auditorium affects sound by making it clear, echoing, warm or muffled and so on.

Composer
Someone who writes music. For some productions, a composer will create original music.

Curtain-call music
Music played during curtain call. Sometimes the curtain call is choreographed to a particular song.

Fade
To gradually turn sound up or down.

Live sounds
Sound created either by the stage management, technicians or actors during the performance. In some productions, where the theatricality of the performance is being highlighted, the sound effects are created in front of the audience.

Microphones
These pick up sound for amplification and might be:
- Body-worn: worn by the actors
- General use: placed near the source of a sound
- Directional: placed at a distance from the source of the sound
- Overheads: hung above the stage to boost the overall sound.

Motivated sound
Sound effects required by the script, particularly in terms of plot and action, such as a gunshot or an alarm.

Musical instruments
Drums, guitars, violins and so on which might be played by a band, orchestra or by the actors.

Musical theme or motif
A distinctive recurring section of music. In sound design, it might be associated with a particular character or mood.

Naturalistic
Realistic sound effects, such as traffic, birdsong, crowds.

Pre-show music
Music played as the audience enters and waits for the performance to begin.

Recorded sound
Played-back sound that might have been recorded specially for the performance or found in sound effects archives.

Reverb
(From 'reverberation'.) An echoing effect, sustaining the sound longer than usual.

Snap
To turn a sound suddenly off or on.

Sound effects (SFX)
Special sounds created either through using recorded effects, such as birdsong and traffic, or creating them live, such as a door slamming or offstage voices.

Speakers
The means of amplifying the sound. The placement of the speakers will influence how the audience experiences the sound.

Transitions/scene changes
How music or sound is used during transitions or scene changes, such as to establish a new location or mood.

Volume
How loud or soft a sound or voice is.

✓ TEST YOURSELF C2

Read these responses to different productions and identify whether they are about **performance**, **sound**, **lighting**, **costume** or **set**. Also consider if they describe, analyse or evaluate.

1 The use of a revolve contributed greatly to the excitement of the party scene. As it slowly turned, the set revealed a new room in the house. As the party continued, the rooms became more and more cluttered, suggesting that the party was getting out of hand.

2 From the actor's first entrance, the audience was captivated. To create the recklessness of his character, he hurtled onto the stage, appearing to be wild and, judging by the bottle he was holding, drunk. He suddenly stopped and smiled slyly, enjoying the impression he had made on both the other characters and the audience.

3 The use of music from the 1950s highlighted the period of the play.

6 A pinpoint spotlight, or pinspot, closed in on the actor's face, showing her distressed expression, followed by a sudden blackout that left the audience shocked.

4 The uniform established the character's status, as well as his appeal to the women of the town. The close-fitting scarlet jacket, with gold braid trim, made him stand out from the other characters who were generally dressed in muted greys, greens and browns.

5 The actors' German accents were truly impressive.

7 As a major theme was women's beauty, the designer had made the three-storey set resemble a beauty counter: white smooth reflective, curved surfaces, racks of pastel products and a large white surface upon which advertisements could be projected.

9 The audience jumped at the unexpected explosion at the end of Act 1. The speakers were positioned all around the auditorium, creating the effect that we too were caught up in the blast.

8 Whenever the children entered, a gentle piece of piano music accompanied them, making their scenes seem almost dream-like.

10 The outfits were stylised and extravagant: primary colours, exaggerated silhouettes and rich fabrics and decorations.

12 A speaker at the back of the auditorium was used to project the sound of a car driving along a gravel drive.

11 Columns of lights descended from the fly space. The mystery of the effect was increased by the use of a haze machine, making the light seem thick, like mist.

 **TEST YOURSELF C3**

Match the correct definition with the technical production term.

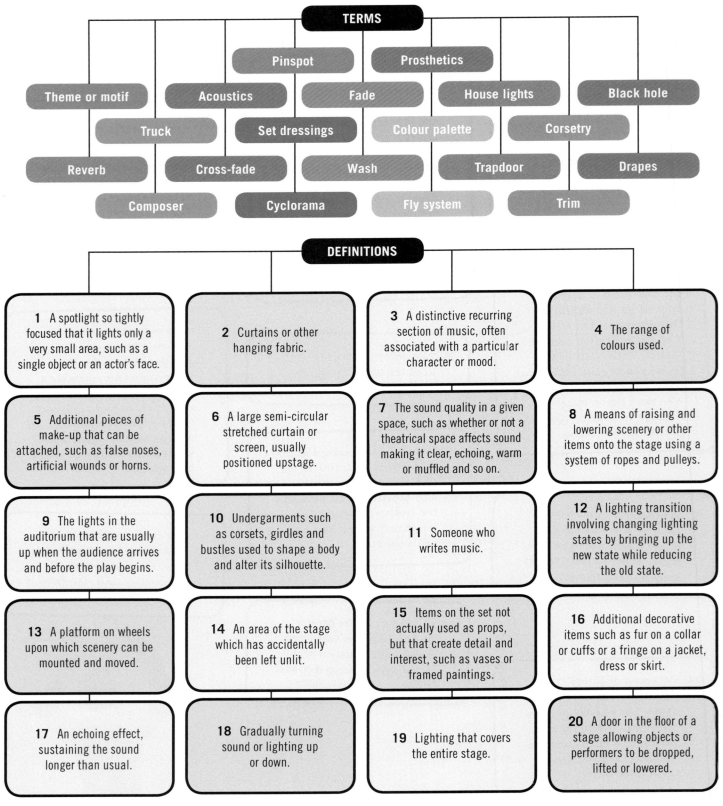

TERMS

- Pinspot
- Prosthetics
- Theme or motif
- Acoustics
- Fade
- House lights
- Black hole
- Truck
- Set dressings
- Colour palette
- Corsetry
- Reverb
- Cross-fade
- Wash
- Trapdoor
- Drapes
- Composer
- Cyclorama
- Fly system
- Trim

DEFINITIONS

1 A spotlight so tightly focused that it lights only a very small area, such as a single object or an actor's face.

2 Curtains or other hanging fabric.

3 A distinctive recurring section of music, often associated with a particular character or mood.

4 The range of colours used.

5 Additional pieces of make-up that can be attached, such as false noses, artificial wounds or horns.

6 A large semi-circular stretched curtain or screen, usually positioned upstage.

7 The sound quality in a given space, such as whether or not a theatrical space affects sound making it clear, echoing, warm or muffled and so on.

8 A means of raising and lowering scenery or other items onto the stage using a system of ropes and pulleys.

9 The lights in the auditorium that are usually up when the audience arrives and before the play begins.

10 Undergarments such as corsets, girdles and bustles used to shape a body and alter its silhouette.

11 Someone who writes music.

12 A lighting transition involving changing lighting states by bringing up the new state while reducing the old state.

13 A platform on wheels upon which scenery can be mounted and moved.

14 An area of the stage which has accidentally been left unlit.

15 Items on the set not actually used as props, but that create detail and interest, such as vases or framed paintings.

16 Additional decorative items such as fur on a collar or cuffs or a fringe on a jacket, dress or skirt.

17 An echoing effect, sustaining the sound longer than usual.

18 Gradually turning sound or lighting up or down.

19 Lighting that covers the entire stage.

20 A door in the floor of a stage allowing objects or performers to be dropped, lifted or lowered.

LEARNING CHECKLIST: SECTION C

Tick each aspect of 'Live theatre production' if you are confident of your knowledge and ability.

If you are unsure of anything, go back and revise.

Do you know...?

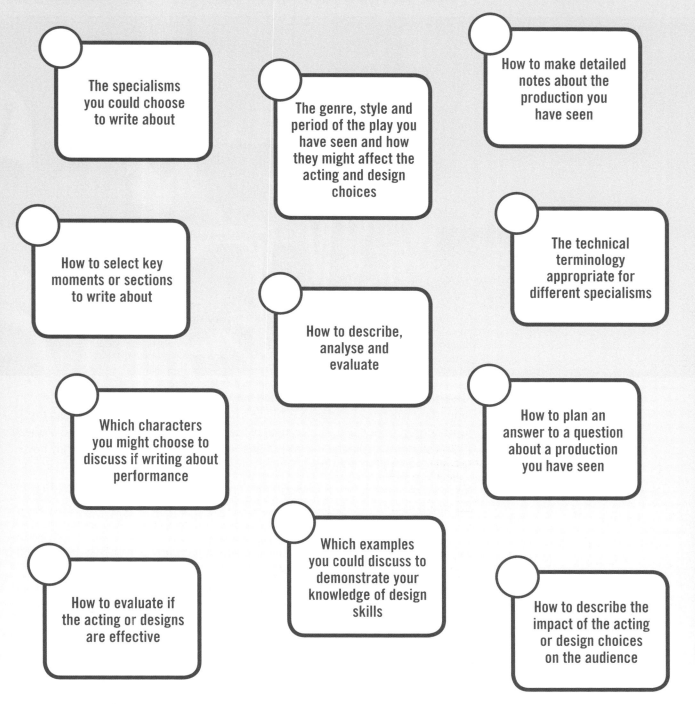

The specialisms you could choose to write about

The genre, style and period of the play you have seen and how they might affect the acting and design choices

How to make detailed notes about the production you have seen

How to select key moments or sections to write about

The technical terminology appropriate for different specialisms

How to describe, analyse and evaluate

Which characters you might choose to discuss if writing about performance

How to plan an answer to a question about a production you have seen

How to evaluate if the acting or designs are effective

Which examples you could discuss to demonstrate your knowledge of design skills

How to describe the impact of the acting or design choices on the audience

How to read the question

The questions in the Drama exam will vary from year to year, but it is always important when you are faced with the exam paper, that you *carefully* read the questions in front of you. In the heat of the moment, it is easy to misread a question. Some students make the mistake of answering a similar question that they have practised for rather than the one which is actually asked.

In order to make sure that you can fully answer a question, you might find the following approach useful.

- Underline key words.
- Double-check any references to a character or particular scenes to ensure that you will write about the correct ones.
- Pay attention to any bullet points. They are there to help you break down and fully grasp the question.
- Make notes around the question if you think straight away of some points you could make.
- As you read the extract given for Section B questions, underline or circle moments that you want to discuss, such as important lines or significant stage directions.

The following pages have example questions with typical points to look out for.

Section B: Study of a set play:
The 39 Steps

1   You are designing a costume ① for Margaret ② to wear in a performance of this extract.③ The costume must reflect the 1930s setting of *The 39 Steps* ④. Describe your design ideas for the costume.

[4 marks]

①   In this case, you are being asked about costume, but the question could have been about other design skills, such as set, lighting or sound.

②   Although there might be several characters in the extract, you must write about Margaret here.

③   Your choices must be appropriate for, and focused on, this particular extract.

④   The context is the 1930s, though there might be variations in how this is worded in the question.

TIP

This question requires a wide range of skills from you, including design and understanding of character, plot and context. It is tempting to spend too long on it, but as it worth relatively few marks, make sure you answer concisely.

2   You are performing the role of Hannay ①.

Describe how you would use your vocal ② and physical ③ skills to perform the line below, and explain the effects ④ you want to create.

'I wish I could take you away from all this!' (page 32) ⑤

[8 marks]

①   Make sure you are writing about the correct character. It is useful to include a sentence about the character and their importance in the play or their emotional state before this line is spoken.

②   Remember that appropriate vocal skills might include volume, accent, pace and emotional range, for example.

③   Physical skills might be gesture, movement, posture, gait, facial expressions.

④   What do you want to achieve? To show that Hannay feels guilty about leaving? That he is attracted to her? What does his delivery of the line tell the audience about him?

TIP

Although worth more marks than Question 1, you must also watch your timing on this question. You might want to aim for two or three vocal skills and two or three physical skills, but avoid over-writing. Remember to both **describe** what you would do and **explain** the effects you hope to achieve.

3 You are performing the role of Margaret. ①

Focus on the shaded part of the extract (page 32, from 'Not that window!' to 'I'm afeart they'll…'). ②

Explain how you and the actor playing Hannay ③ might use the performance space ④ and interact ⑤ with each other to show the audience the tense and romantic relationship ⑥ between the characters.

[12 marks]

① Again, make sure you are writing about the correct character.

② In the exam paper, the area to focus on will be shaded in grey and is included as part of a longer extract.

③ You should make reference to the other character and their actions in relation to your character.

④ Where are you positioned on the stage? When and where might you move? Will your proximity to each other change?

⑤ How do you respond to each other? Do you react at a particular moment? Is there any physical contact or change in facial expression?

⑥ In this instance, you are being asked to look at how a tense and romantic relationship is created. On other papers you might be looking at creating a particular mood, style or emotion, such as conflict or comedy.

TIP

When writing responses to acting questions like this, it is a good idea to write in the first person, so 'As Margaret, I am attracted to Hannay and frightened of my husband, so I will…'

4 You are performing the role of Richard Hannay. ①

Describe how you would use your acting skills ② to portray Hannay's character.

Explain why your ideas ③ are appropriate for:

- This extract (page 41) ④
- The performance of your role in the play as a whole. ⑤

[20 marks]

① Typically, Question 4 will focus on a different character in the extract from the one that was the focus for Question 3.

② Acting skills, unless otherwise specified, should include vocal and physical skills.

③ Consider your understanding of the character, their motivations and role in the play and how these ideas can be practically realised in performance.

④ You might want to focus on particular lines or stage directions from the extract in order to provide precise details.

⑤ You could choose two or three moments from other sections of the play and describe and analyse acting choices that could be made. Does the character change and develop, or are they consistent throughout?

TIP

Remember to use the correct acting terminology when writing about your acting choices. This is a good opportunity to demonstrate how your acting skills can convey the character's mental state, social status, development and importance to the play as a whole.

5 You are a designer working on one aspect of design ① for this extract. Describe ② how you would use your design skills to create effects ③ which support the action of this extract. ④ Explain why your ideas are appropriate for this extract and the play as a whole. ⑤ [20 marks]

① Note that you are to choose one design specialism to write about: lighting, costume, set, sound or puppetry.

② Describe in detail, with correct terminology, your ideas for the extract.

③ What impact will your design choices have, for example creating a certain mood or location, or enhancing a certain aspect of a character?

④ Specify how your design is appropriate for the particular scene given.

⑤ Provide practical examples of how your ideas can work in the rest of the play too.

TIP

Remember that you will answer *either* Question 4 or Question 5.

TIP

Question 4 or Question 5 is worth the most marks in Section B, so make sure you allow the most time to answer it.

Section C: Understanding drama: Live theatre production

Performance

Describe ① how an actor used their acting skills ② to create an effective character ③ within the production. Analyse ④ and evaluate ⑤ how successful they were in communicating their role to the audience. ⑥

You could make reference to:

- Vocal skills, such as tone, accent, pace, pitch and emotional range ⑦
- Physical skills, such as gestures and movement ⑧
- A scene or key moments from the whole play. ⑨ [32 marks]

① Be clear when describing the performance because it is unlikely the examiner will have seen the same performance. You might be asked to describe a single character or you might have the option to write about several.

② Unless otherwise specified, this should include vocal and physical skills.

③ Another exam paper might ask something different, such as, how the role was conveyed to an audience or how convincing a performance was.

④ Break down the specifics of the performance.

⑤ Did the performance work? If so, why? If not, why not?

⑥ What impact did the performance have on the audience?

⑦ Bullet points provide helpful prompts, but don't be restricted by them if you want to discuss other vocal skills, for example.

⑧ Depending on the performance, you could discuss other physical skills.

⑨ You might be prompted to look at a scene or section, key moments or the play as a whole. It is a good idea to prepare in advance several sections or moments you could write about, then make your final choices based on the question before you.

Design

Ray Fearon and Tara Fitzgerald in Macbeth *at the Globe, in costumes designed by Joan O'Clery* ▲

Describe how costumes ① were used to support the style ② of the production. Analyse and evaluate how successful ③ the costumes were in helping to convey the style to the audience. ④

You could make reference to:

- The fabrics and other materials used ⑤
- The colour and textures used ⑥
- Hair, make-up and accessories ⑦
- A scene or the production as a whole. ⑧   [32 marks]

① The design specialism is identified as costume in this section and the plural word 'costumes' indicates, in this case, that you should describe more than one, if possible.

② The style of the production could involve a discussion on whether the costumes are realistic and naturalistic, symbolic, comic or representative of a particular period. Other papers might ask you to focus on whether the costumes help to convey characterisation and/or the action and plot of the play.

③ You must remember to evaluate the costumes, judging if they worked well and if so, why, and if not, why not.

④ This invites you to discuss the impact on the audience, for example, the first impression a costume created or if a costume showed a character or situation developing or changing.

⑤ This bullet point is a helpful prompt, but, depending on the production you have seen, you might have additional points you wish to make.

⑥ Remember to use correct costume terminology throughout. Although this prompt asks about colour, simply writing that a character 'wears a red dress' won't gain you many marks. Look for more details and technical features.

⑦ Precise details about these could boost your marks.

⑧ In this case, you are being given the choice of a scene — the length of which you may choose yourself — or the whole play. If you write about the whole play, choose a few key costumes rather than spreading yourself too thinly.

TIP

Typically, Section C will have one acting question and two questions on named design specialisms. You cannot assume that any specific question will be asked. You might only prepare, say, a lighting question, but find when you open the paper that lighting is not one of the specialisms named.

TIP

Section C has the single question worth the most marks, so make sure you allow enough time for it.

Making plans

You will need to be aware of timing in the exam, and you will probably find that you have relatively little time for planning. It is certainly worth, however, taking a couple of minutes to plan for some of the questions worth the most marks, such as Section B Questions 4 or 5 or your choice of question in Section C.

The following are a few brief suggestions of how to make a plan.

TIP

Make clear which design specialism you have chosen for this question.

Annotating the question

You could note some key words around the question as you read it, for example:

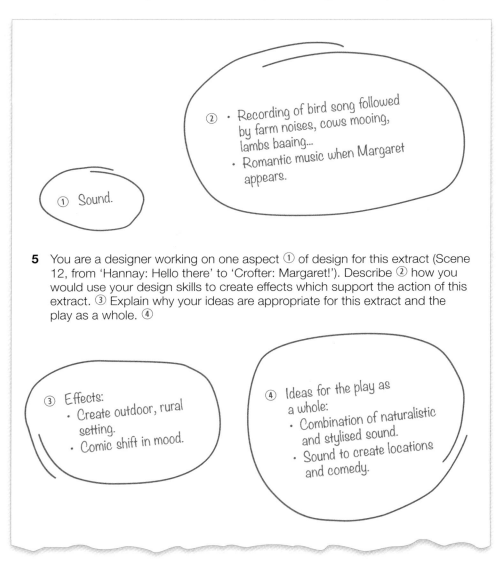

① Sound.

② • Recording of bird song followed by farm noises, cows mooing, lambs baaing…
• Romantic music when Margaret appears.

5 You are a designer working on one aspect ① of design for this extract (Scene 12, from 'Hannay: Hello there' to 'Crofter: Margaret!'). Describe ② how you would use your design skills to create effects which support the action of this extract. ③ Explain why your ideas are appropriate for this extract and the play as a whole. ④

③ Effects:
• Create outdoor, rural setting.
• Comic shift in mood.

④ Ideas for the play as a whole:
• Combination of naturalistic and stylised sound.
• Sound to create locations and comedy.

A mind map

Another flexible and quick way of drawing up a plan is to create a mind map. For example, for **costumes** for the Crofter and Hannay:

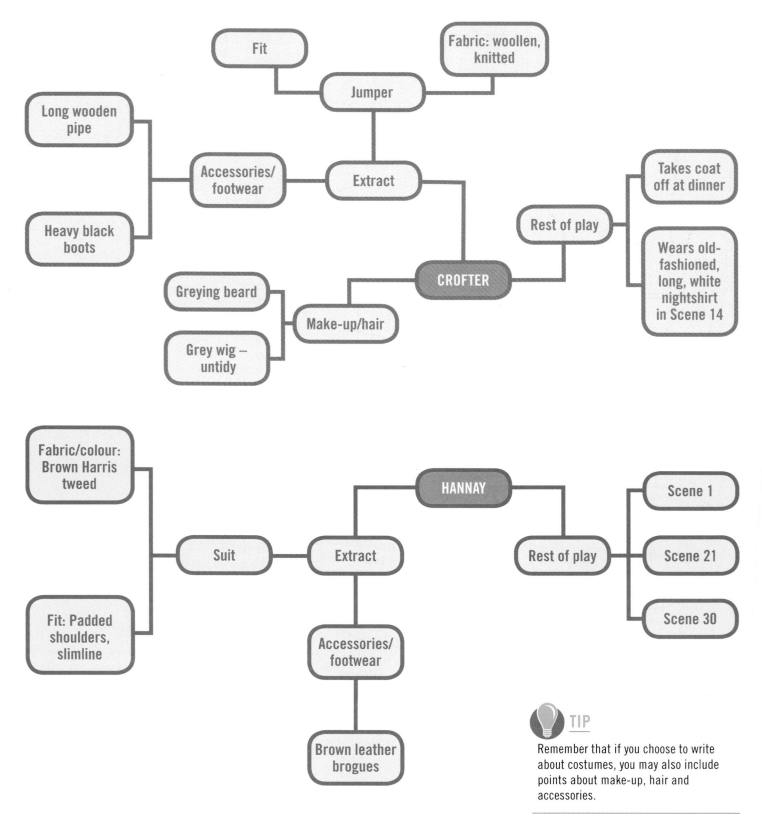

TIP

Remember that if you choose to write about costumes, you may also include points about make-up, hair and accessories.

Lists

After you have read through a question, you could quickly make a list of points you want to make and then go back and tick off the items once you have included them in your answer.

 TIP

Remember that, if it helps you, you can draw a quick sketch to clarify your design ideas as part of your answer. For example, the Crofter:

Acting the Crofter

This extract: Scene 12

Physical:

- Gait/stance: Walks with a limp and stands with legs wide apart, looking combative.
- Gestures: Holds a wooden smoking pipe that he gestures with when he talks.
- Pace: Slow, pauses before, 'Oh that big house.'
- Eye contact: Peers suspiciously at Hannay, narrows eyes.

Vocal:

- Volume: Moderately loud – perhaps hard of hearing?
- Accent: Strong Highlands accent.
- Emotional range: Angry, suspicious, snaps in annoyance.

Rest of play:

In Scene 13, Crofter attempts to dominate and interrupt.

- Pace: quick, dramatic entrance.
- Volume: Loud, changes mood of scene.
- Facial expression: Alert when examining Hannay, but closes his eyes during prayer.
- Comically positioned between Margaret and Hannay.

In Scene 14: Highly agitated, accuses Hannay.

- Volume: Shouts.
- Physical movements: Runs between window, door and Hannay and Margaret. Suddenly stops at the mention of money.

Action of play:

- Crofter is an obstacle to Hannay's escape and in his relationship with Margaret.
- He is a comic, exaggerated character.

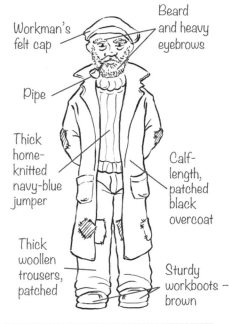

Workman's felt cap
Beard and heavy eyebrows
Pipe
Thick home-knitted navy-blue jumper
Calf-length, patched black overcoat
Thick woollen trousers, patched
Sturdy workboots – brown

 **LOOK HERE**

See pages 76 and 85 for other examples of planning an exam response.

Shaping and improving the quality of your writing

Well-organised and clearly developed writing makes a positive impression and will help you to avoid common exam mistakes, such as drifting off topic or repeating yourself.

Some ideas for improving your answers include:

▸ Use some of the wording from the question. For example, if the question asks you to use your skills to 'create tension', make sure that the phrase appears at least once (and probably more frequently) in your response.

▸ Think about the order in which you write about your ideas. You might quickly number any ideas in any plans you have made in order to confirm the order.

▸ Check over your work to make sure you have answered each aspect of the question. You might use your plan or the bullet points provided in some questions and tick these off once you have written about them.

 TIP

Avoid over-writing on questions only worth a few marks. If there are only four marks available for a question, no matter how much or how brilliantly you write, you will not be awarded more than that.

Using discursive markers

Discursive markers are phrases that you can use to link, order or otherwise clarify your ideas. Think of them as signposts which help the reader to understand in what order you want them to consider your ideas or which ideas are to be contrasted or highlighted. Use of discursive markers can give you writing a better flow and make it easier to understand, as well as helping you to express more sophisticated ideas.

Some examples of discursive markers include:

Ordering
first, second, to begin, initially, next, finally, ultimately, in conclusion

Emphasising
most importantly, significantly, remarkably

Comparing and contrasting
similarly, in contrast, both, in the same way, rather than

Providing examples
for instance, for example, in this case

Building an argument
additionally, in addition, another

Providing contrasting points of view
however, but, in spite of this

Task 1

Read this excerpt from a student-style answer and underline or highlight each example of a discursive marker.

> Initially, the sound designer used a range of recorded and live sound effects in order to create a sense of menace. An example of this was the contrasting use of recorded classical music with the sudden offstage sound of breaking glass. In addition, she experimented with the location of the sounds, some seeming to come from behind or to the sides of the audience, while others clearly originated from the stage. However, the effect was not always successful because of the low volume used.

Task 2

Write a paragraph about a production you have seen. In it, introduce at least three discursive markers to clarify your ideas.

Checking your work for typical errors

Every year, there are some common errors made in the exam, costing students marks. Below are some examples and possible solutions.

Running out of time

The exam lasts 1 hour and 45 minutes and is worth 80 marks in total. You need to allow time for reading the questions and extract, planning your response and checking your work, so that means you have only a little more than a minute per mark of writing time. Therefore, you need to use your time wisely. Here are some suggestions for good time-keeping:

▸ Practise working on a real examination question paper, making sure you can quickly locate the questions you need to answer.

▸ Practise writing to a time limit. Some students find it helpful early in the course to write untimed responses so that they can thoroughly explore their ideas, but gradually introduce writing to a fixed time, so, by the time they come to the exam, they are very used to the correct timings.

▸ Think about the order in which you complete the questions. You can answer them in any order. Some students prefer to undertake the examination in the order that the questions are asked, using the low-mark questions as a warm up and confidence-builder before answering the questions that are worth more marks. Alternatively, you might start with the questions worth the most marks. Some students choose to answer the questions in reverse, starting with Section C and finishing with Section A.

▸ Make sure, however, that you answer every question. If you leave out, for example, Section C or a valuable question from Section B, it will cost you dearly.

TIP

As you prepare and practise in the build up to the exam, it is worth experimenting with different timings. Make sure that you are able to answer all of the questions fully in the time allowed.

TIP

This is not an exam where you should expect to have any time left over at the end. There is no advantage to completing your work early.

▸ Plan how long you will spend on each section. There is no set way of doing this, but here is an example of one candidate's plan that you might find useful:

– Section A: 5 minutes
– Section B: 50 minutes
– Section C: 40 minutes
– Reading/checking: 10 minutes.

Writing that is too general

Although you might have very strong ideas of what you want to achieve through your use of acting or design, you must make sure that you present these ideas in a precise and clear way.

Task 3

Read the candidate-style response about the lighting for the final scene of *The 39 Steps*. After reading the annotation questions to prompt improvement, rewrite the paragraph with more precise details.

> I want the lighting to look very happy and bright. ① This will be from the lighting in the wings and fly space. ② There will be a Christmas tree on stage with sparkling fairy lights. ③ The two Clown actors will be standing on a ladder and I will have a spotlight on them. When Pamela and Hannay kiss, there will be a spotlight on them as well. ④

① What will the lighting state be here? A blackout? A fade up? How will you transition to it looking happy and bright?

② What colour will the light be? What angle will it be? How bright? How will it be produced? (What type of lantern?)

③ How will the lights on the tree come on? Will someone on stage turn them on, or will they be operated by a technician? Will they flash, twinkle or be just a steady light? Will they be one colour or multi-coloured?

④ What colours and size will the spotlights be? What effects are you creating by using the spotlights?

Omitting technical terms

Technical vocabulary is important in showing that you understand the different aspects, skills and techniques of live theatre. Failing to use them in an exam response might suggest that there are gaps in your learning or understanding.

TIP

Remember that the Section C question will not provide the name of the production you saw, so don't waste time looking for it. Also remember that your Section C play cannot be the same as your Section B set text.

TIP

Try to locate particular moments or particular lines of dialogue when effects might occur.

Task 4

Read the following responses about the performance of Pamela in the scene on pages 21–22. Locate technical terminology used.

Which do you think is the more effective answer? Why?

Pamela is the love interest, but also is frequently in conflict with Hannay. This scene is when the audience first sees her, so I want to show that she is intelligent, attractive and independent. I will move in slow motion when I 'remove my glasses' and put down my book. I will then suggest a transformation to a more glamorous character, by letting down my hair and gazing dreamily out of the window. When Hannay sweeps into the compartment and kisses me, it will be unclear from my body language whether or not I am pleased about this. Our proximity will be very close, and it is only when we pull apart that the audience will see my shocked facial expression – mouth and eyes both wide open in horror. The originally dreamy impression of me will contrast with my cut-glass, authoritative English accent when I say, 'This is the man you want Inspector.' I will speak loudly with a tone of outrage and point at Hannay.

Pamela is a very beautiful woman and the audience must understand that she is very attractive. As Pamela, I will strike a number of appealing poses. When Hannay comes in and kisses me, I will have no choice but to go along with it, but, when I finally speak, the audience will be able to tell I wasn't happy because I identify him to the police. I will have an English accent and speak in a reasonable tone. I will perform a variety of gestures, such as pointing and crossing my arms. It is important that the audience think that we look good together but also sense that I am not easily won over by his actions.

 TIP

It might seem obvious, but make sure that in Section B you answer about the set text you have studied in Drama. Every year, there are students who write about another play, such as one they have studied in English. The demands of English and Drama are different, and, for the Drama exam, you will need to write about the play you have studied on your Drama course.

Task 5

Choose another scene between Pamela and Hannay and discuss how you would perform Pamela. Use technical terminology whenever you can.

Sample question paper

For practice, you might like to attempt this exam paper under timed exam conditions.

Section A: Theatre roles and terminology

1 In the professional theatre, who is responsible for operating the technical equipment such as the sound board?

    A The sound designer.

    B The stage manager.

    C The technician.   [1 mark]

2 When performing in a promenade production, which of the following do you need to consider?

    A How you will use the proscenium and apron area of the stage.

    B The health and safety of the audience as they follow the actors around the set.

    C Where to store large set items in the theatre's wings.   [1 mark]

3 What type of stage is shown in Figure 1?

    A A proscenium arch.

    B A thrust stage.

    C A traverse stage.   [1 mark]

4 In Figure 1, where is the table located?

    A Downstage right.

    B Centre stage left.

    C Downstage left.   [1 mark]

Figure 1

Section B: Study of a Set Play: *The 39 Steps*

Focus on an extract from Scene 3, pages 6–7, from 'Annabella: Turn it off! Quickly!' to 'Annabella: Please don't answer!!!'

5.1 You are designing the setting for a performance of this extract. The setting must reflect the 1930s period setting of *The 39 Steps*. Describe your design ideas for the setting.   [4 marks]

5.2 You are performing the role of Annabella.

Describe how you would use your vocal and physical skills to perform the line below, and explain the effects you want to create.

'Turn it off! Quickly!'   [8 marks]

5.3 You are performing the role of Annabella.

Focus on 'Annabella: Now the light Mr Hannay!' to 'Hannay: Hello. There's the telephone.'

Explain how you and the actor playing Hannay might use the performance space and interact with each other to establish tension for the audience.   [12 marks]

And EITHER

5.4 You are performing the role of Hannay.

Describe how you would use your acting skills to interpret Hannay's character in this extract, and explain why your ideas are appropriate both for this extract and the play as a whole. [20 marks]

OR

5.5 You are a designer working on one aspect of design for this extract.

Describe how you would use your design skills to create effects which support the action of this extract, and explain why your ideas are appropriate both for this extract and the play as a whole. [20 marks]

Section C: Live theatre production

Answer **one** question from this section.

State the title of the live theatre production you saw:

10 Describe how one actor in the play you saw used their acting skills to create an appropriate and interesting character. Analyse and evaluate how successful they were in communicating their character to the audience.

You should make reference to:
- The actor's use of the performance space
- The actor's use of vocal and physical skills
- The actor's understanding of the character's motivations and background
- A scene/section or the whole play. [32 marks]

OR

11 Describe how lighting was used to support the style and context of the production. Analyse and evaluate how successful the lighting design was in communicating the meaning and mood of the production to the audience.

You could make reference to:
- Colours and intensity
- Any transitions
- Any special effects
- A section of the play or the whole play. [32 marks]

OR

12 Describe how costumes were used to enhance the characterisations of one or more characters in the play. Analyse and evaluate how successful the costumes were in helping to communicate the character's or characters' importance in the action of the play and any changes or development they undergo.

You could make reference to:
- The materials used
- The shape/fit/silhouette
- The colour/texture.
- A scene or the play or the play as a whole. [32 marks]

TIP

Section B in the exam consists of Questions 5 to 10, including questions about the other set texts. You will need to locate the set of questions relevant to *The 39 Steps*.

LEARNING CHECKLIST: EXAMINATION PRACTICE

Tick each aspect of exam preparation if you are confident of your knowledge.

If you are unsure of anything, read through this section again.

Do you know...?

How to look for key words in the questions

The difference between your Section B and Section C texts

How to avoid running out of time

How to include detail and refer to specific examples

How to plan an answer

How to use discursive markers

How to include technical terminology

The range of questions you could be asked

www.illuminatepublishing.com/drama

Answers to 'Test yourself' questions

Test yourself 1 (page 5)

1   Section C.

2   4.

3   Section B.

4   40 per cent.

5   Section A.

6   The glossary.

Test yourself A2 (page 12)

1   Traverse.

2   Promenade.

3   End on.

Test yourself A3 (page 19)

A   Thrust.

B   End on.

C   Traverse.

D   Theatre in the round.

E   Promenade.

F   Proscenium arch.

Test yourself A1 (page 9) ▼

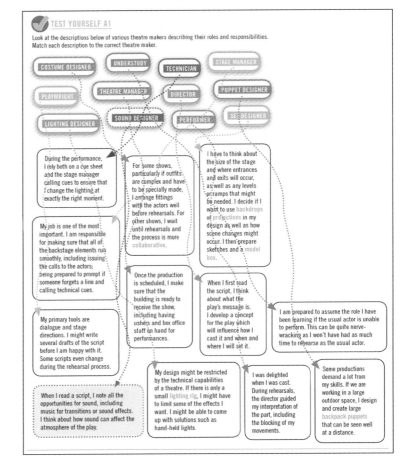

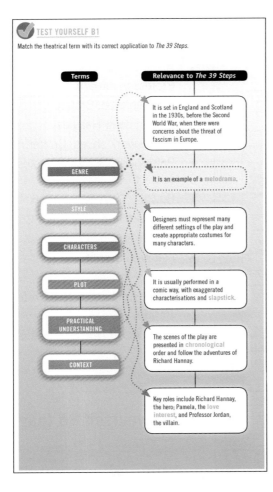

◀ **Test yourself B1 (page 23)**

Test yourself B2 (page 27)

1 Policeman, Scene 8.
2 Milkman, Scene 5.
3 Crofter, Scene 13.
4 Hannay, Scene 3.
5 Mrs Jordan, Scene 17.
6 Pamela, Scene 9.
7 Margaret, Scene 13.
8 Annabella, Scene 3.
9 Mrs McGarrigle, Scene 28.
10 Margaret, Scene 14.
11 Professor Jordan, Scene 18
12 Hannay, Scene 21.
13 Pamela, Scene 25.
14 Pamela, Scene 29.
15 Mr Memory, Scene 31.

Test yourself B3 (page 31)

1 1935.
2 Through her accent.
3 A jitterbug.
4 In the newspaper and on radio broadcasts.
5 Suspender belt, flat cap, pencil skirt, Harris tweed, trilbies.
6 There is a fear of a foreign/enemy power (Germany) threatening Britain.

Test yourself B4 (page 35)

▸ Black dress shoes: Professor Jordan.
▸ Coarse tweed waistcoat: Crofter.
▸ Long, black, wool coat, patched: Crofter.
▸ Black trousers with a centre crease: Professor Jordan.
▸ Wooden pipe: Crofter.
▸ Trench coat: Heavies.
▸ Heavy work shoes: Crofter.
▸ Patterned silk cravat: Professor Jordan.
▸ Bow tie: Professor Jordan.
▸ Hand-knitted wool scarf: Crofter.
▸ Brown brogues: Heavies.
▸ Flat cap: Crofter.
▸ Trilby: Heavies.
▸ Velvet smoking jacket: Professor Jordan.
▸ Blue tie: Heavies.

◀ Test yourself B5 (page 47)

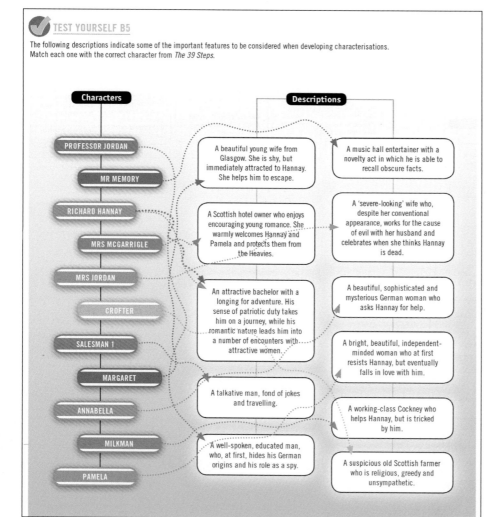

TEST YOURSELF B5

The following descriptions indicate some of the important features to be considered when developing characterisations. Match each one with the correct character from *The 39 Steps*.

Characters
- PROFESSOR JORDAN
- MR MEMORY
- RICHARD HANNAY
- MRS MCGARRIGLE
- MRS JORDAN
- CROFTER
- SALESMAN 1
- MARGARET
- ANNABELLA
- MILKMAN
- PAMELA

Descriptions
- A beautiful young wife from Glasgow. She is shy, but immediately attracted to Hannay. She helps him to escape.
- A music hall entertainer with a novelty act in which he is able to recall obscure facts.
- A Scottish hotel owner who enjoys encouraging young romance. She warmly welcomes Hannay and Pamela and protects them from the Heavies.
- A 'severe-looking' wife who, despite her conventional appearance, works for the cause of evil with her husband and celebrates when she thinks Hannay is dead.
- An attractive bachelor with a longing for adventure. His sense of patriotic duty takes him on a journey, while his romantic nature leads him into a number of encounters with attractive women.
- A beautiful, sophisticated and mysterious German woman who asks Hannay for help.
- A bright, beautiful, independent-minded woman who at first resists Hannay, but eventually falls in love with him.
- A talkative man, fond of jokes and travelling.
- A working-class Cockney who helps Hannay, but is tricked by him.
- A well-spoken, educated man, who, at first, hides his German origins and his role as a spy.
- A suspicious old Scottish farmer who is religious, greedy and unsympathetic.

Test yourself B6 (page 53) ▶

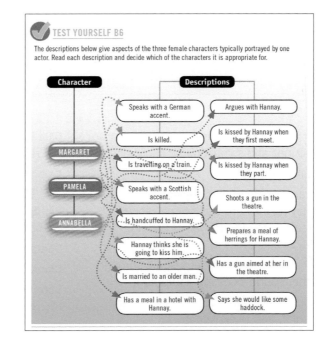

Test yourself B7 (page 55)

1   Mrs Jordan.
2   Mrs Jordan.
3   The Professor.
4   The Professor.
5   The Professor.
6   Mrs Jordan.
7   The Professor.
8   Mrs Jordan.
9   The Professor.
10 The Professor.

Test yourself B8 (page 88) ▶

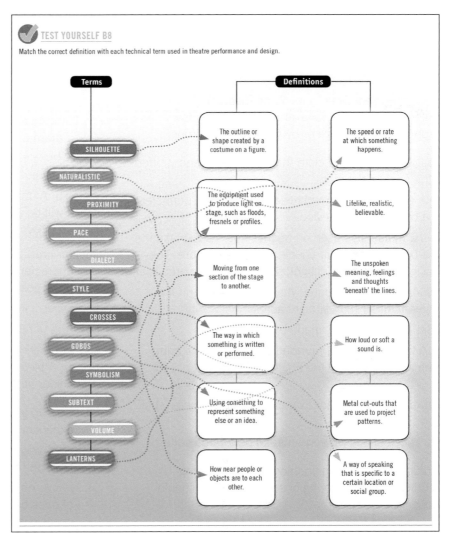

GLOSSARY

Abstract: Not realistic or lifelike; instead using colours, shapes, textures, sounds and so on for a symbolic effect.

Affluent: Wealthy, prosperous, well off.

Alienation effect: A distancing effect that prevents the audience from believing they are watching a real event. It might involve breaking the fourth wall or drawing attention to the play's mechanics of production.

Amplification: How sounds are made louder, usually through microphones or other sound-boosting equipment.

Analyse: To examine something, perhaps by looking at the different elements of it, and to explain it.

Antagonist: A character who opposes, works against or brings down the protagonist.

Apron: The front area of the stage, nearest the audience, which projects in front of the curtain.

Asymmetrical: Having two sides that do not match, or something that leans to one side.

Audience interaction: Directly involving members of the audience in the play, for example by asking for a response from onstage or by passing them props.

Backdrop: A large painted cloth that serves as scenery, often at the back of the stage.

Backpack puppets: Large puppets attached to the puppeteer by a backpack-like device.

Barn doors: Metal flaps used on fresnel lanterns to make the light beam a particular shape, such as a square. They also lessen the 'spill' of light, so that a precise area is lit.

Bias-cut: A tailoring technique where fabric is cut on the diagonal rather than straight across.

Block: Set the movements made by the actors.

Bowler: A black hat with a rounded top and a small brim, often associated with the English 'city gent'.

Box set: A set with three complete walls, often used in naturalistic designs, for example to create a believable room.

Brogues: Laced shoes with ornamental perforated patterns.

Call the cues: Announce instructions, such as telling technicians when lighting or sound changes should occur.

Camiknickers: A one-piece undergarment that combines the top of a slip or camisole with a pair of French knickers.

Catalyst: Something or someone who starts a reaction or triggers events.

Chairography: Choreographed movement involving moving or rearranging chairs on stage.

Characters: The people involved in the action of a story.

Charlady: A cleaning woman.

Chronological: Events presented in the order in which they occurred.

Climax: The moment of highest tension, usually of great importance and often the culmination of earlier events.

Collaborative: A process where people work together rather than individually.

Colour palette: The range of colours used, such as light colours, dark colours, earth tones, muted tones or vivid, primary colours.

Comic relief: Light-hearted characters or interludes that provide a break from more intense, serious sections of a drama.

Composite set: A single set that represents several locations at once.

Concept: A unifying idea about the production, such as how it will be interpreted and performed.

Cross: Movement from one section of the stage to another.

Counter-cross: Movement in opposition to another character's cross, so, one going stage left when the other goes stage right.

Court shoes: Plain strapless shoes with a raised heel.

Covering (a role): Learning the lines and movements for a part that you do not usually perform.

Cravat: A piece of fabric, wider than a tie, usually in a bold colour or pattern, tucked into a shirt collar.

Describe: To give details of what you saw, heard or experienced.

Dialect: A way of speaking that is specific to a certain location or social group.

Dicky bow: An informal term for a bow tie, which is a type of neck tie shaped into a bow, usually worn on formal occasions.

Distressed: When furniture or objects have been treated in order to look old or weathered.

Double act: Two performers who work closely together.

Double-breasted: A coat or jacket with two lines of buttons down the front rather than one.

Double-take: To look at something once, then realise what you have seen and immediately look a second time; a comic technique that indicates a sense of surprise.

End on: A staging configuration in which the audience sits along one end of the stage (the front), directly facing it.

Entourage: A group of people who escort or assist an important person.

Epic: A type of early 20th-century theatre particularly associated with Bertolt Brecht. It is non-naturalistic and uses particular techniques to remind the audience they are watching a play.

Expressionistic: A non-naturalistic style that highlights subjective emotions.

Evaluate: To judge or form an opinion, such as explaining what effect was created and how successful it was.

Fascism: A dictatorial form of government with extreme, intolerant views and practices.

Fedora: A hat that resembles a trilby, but with a wider brim.

Flats: Pieces of scenery mounted on frames, for example representing walls.

Fly space: The area above the stage where scenery might be stored and lowered to the stage.

Fogger: A device that produces a smoke that gives the effect of fog or mist.

Followspot: A powerful spotlight operated so that its beam follows an actor around the stage.

Fourth wall: An imaginary wall that separates the actors from the audience, giving the impression that the world of the actors is entirely distinct from that of the audience.

Fresnel: A lantern with a lens that produces a soft-edged beam of light.

Front of house: Ushers and other members of theatre staff who deal with the audience, as opposed to those who work backstage.

Gait: A way of walking.

Genre: A category or type of music, art or literature, usually with its own typical conventions.

Girdle: An undergarment in a stretchy fabric that gives a slim, smoothe silhouette to waist and hips.

Gobo: A metal cut-out used to project patterns, such as leaves, stars, swirls or waves.

Harris tweed: An exclusive, high-quality, handwoven, woollen cloth.

Herringbone: A pattern made up of rows of 'v' shapes.

Immersive: A type of theatre where the audience are in the middle of the action, without the sense of separation usually associated with going to the theatre.

Interpretation: Bringing out a particular meaning by making specific choices – in this case, choices about how a play could be performed and designed.

Intonation: The rise and fall of pitch in the voice; the musicality of speech.

Kitten heel: A shoe with a low, narrow, curved heel, often open at the back, with a strap.

Lighting plot: A guide to the lighting of a production, including the locations and types of lighting instruments and a scene-by-scene list of requirements.

Lighting rig: The structure that holds the lighting equipment in the theatre (usually in the roof).

Lighting states: The settings and positions of lighting to create certain conditions, such as a bright afternoon or a moonlit scene.

Love interest: A character whose primary importance is their romantic relationship with a central character.

Marionette: A puppet worked by strings.

Melodrama: A type of drama with exaggerated characters and exciting events.

Mime: To act without words, or to use movement, gesture and expression to create objects or a narrative.

Minimalist: Simple, spare; using few elements.

Model box: A three-dimensional scale-model of the set that shows how the real set will look and work.

Motivations: The feelings behind what a character wants or needs.

Multi-role: One actor playing more than one character.

Musical: A type of play in which music, singing and dancing play a significant part.

Naturalistic: Lifelike, believable, realistic.

Oxfords: Plain, formal, lace-up shoes.

Pace: The speed or rate at which something happens.

Parody: An exaggerated, but sometimes affectionate, imitation made for comic effect.

Phrasing: How the words in a line of speech are grouped together, such as said on a single breath or broken into fragments.

Pinspot: A spotlight so tightly focused it only lights a very small area.

Pitch: How high or low a voice is.

Plot: The sequence of main events of a play, film or novel.

Practical: Something that can actually be physically done, rather than simply an idea.

Pristine: As if new; perfect; clean.

Projections: A technique where moving or still images are projected to form a theatrical backdrop.

Prompt book: A copy of the production script of the play, which includes detailed information about the play's blocking, props and other technical elements.

Props: Small items that actors can carry, such as books, a pistol or a bottle.

Protagonist: The leading character in a play.

Proximity: How near people or objects are to each other; also referred to as 'proxemics', which describes the relative positions of characters on stage.

Register: The vocal range of the voice (upper, middle or lower register) and the variety of tones of voice.

Resolution: The point at which most plot elements have been settled.

Rhetorical questions: Questions that do not demand an answer as it is already implied, but are asked for effect or to make a point.

Serif: A style of typeface that has additional decorations beyond the basic letters.

Set dressings: Items on the set not used as props, but which create detail and interest in it.

Sightlines: The view the audience has of the stage and/or action.

Silhouette: The outline or shape of a figure.

Slapstick: Broad physical comedy, including chase scenes and exaggerated fights and tumbles.

Sound plot: A list of the sound effects or music needed and sound equipment that will be used. This is usually organised scene-by-scene and contains information such as cues and volume.

Stage picture: A well-arranged stage image that conveys a certain impression to the audience; also called a 'tableau'.

Staging configuration: The type of stage and audience arrangement.

Status: The social or professional standing of a person.

Still image: An acting technique when the actors freeze a moment in silence, showing the characters' positions and expressions.

Strobe: A lighting device that produces short bursts of light.

Style: The way in which something is created or performed.

Stylised: Non-realistic, heightened, exaggerated; done in a manner that perhaps emphasises one element.

Subliminally: In a way that barely registers: the audience is affected without being conscious of what is affecting them.

Subplot: A secondary storyline, less important than the main plot.

Subtext: The unspoken meaning, feelings and thoughts 'beneath' the lines.

Symbolic: Using something to represent something else. A symbolic stage design, for example, might be non-naturalistic to suggest something about the play's themes.

Synchronised: Something done at the same time as someone or something else is doing the same. Synchronised movement or speech in theatre is when characters move or speak in unison.

Thrillers: Books, plays or films that create excitement and suspense with plots that usually involve crime and deception.

Top hat: A formal hat, usually in a smooth black fabric, which has a tall, cylindrical shape and a brim.

Tragicomic: A creative work, such as a play or novel, with both tragic and comic elements.

Trench coat: A belted raincoat, usually beige or tan.

Trilby: A soft, narrow-brimmed felt hat.

Truck: A platform on wheels upon which scenery can be mounted and moved.

Tweed: A thick wool fabric of more than one colour.

Virtuoso: Highly skilled; expert in an artistic skill, such as music, dance or acting.

Wing space: An unseen area to the side of the stage where actors wait to enter and where props and set pieces can be stored.